Now Is the Time to Leave Public Schools

Stasia Decker-Ahmed

ISBN number: 978-1-7345634-8-1

Disclaimer: I am not an attorney, nor do I have any legal degrees. The information in this book is from my professional and personal experience as well as my own research and should not be taken as legal or financial advice.

Dedicated to children everywhere, and those who desire to provide them with the best education possible.

Contents

Introduction

During the 1970s and 80s, I attended school when there weren't metal detectors on the doors, police officers patrolling the parking lot, and school shootings were virtually unheard of. Most kids graduated with adequate reading, writing, and math skills. The values taught in school were similar to those held by parents and the local community.

Public education has changed dramatically since I was in school in the previous century. There have been even more changes in just the last few years that have negatively affected not only how children are educated but also the current state of our society.

The results have been nothing short of disastrous. Millions of students go through the public school system, yet many are functionally illiterate. They can't adequately fill out a job application, write a coherent paragraph, or complete basic math functions. And these are just the academic problems.

Public schools have been promoting a humanist, socialist agenda for years. Bullying, violence, and school shootings are rampant. Many schools are now teaching gender identity as early as kindergarten. Schools are crowded, teachers are overworked, and even the "good suburban schools" are not immune to many of these problems, including the overwhelming influence of teachers' unions.

These changes have sent millions of American families running for the public school doors. Even before the COVID-19 pandemic, parents were increasingly growing discontent with public education. Since the pandemic, however, many parents realized they could successfully educate their children outside the government-run school system. Many more would like to do it but are not sure how.

This book is a how-to guide for those wanting to provide the best education possible for their children. It is divided into twelve chapters.

Chapter One discusses what is currently happening in public education and the many reasons why parents, if they have not already decided to do so, should seriously consider educational alternatives for their children. Chapter Two explains the different options available. Chapter Three explains how a family can set up a homeschool. Chapter Four provides advice on how parents can work with their church to either start a parochial school or partner with the church for homeschooling. Chapter Five discusses how and why churches should be involved in educating children.

In Chapter Six, I explain the various laws and regulations involved in leaving public schools and starting different educational options. Chapter Seven provides guidelines for what children should learn at each stage of the educational process. Chapter Eight offers specific tips for how parents can afford to leave public schools.

Chapter Nine explains how local communities can support homeschooling and other alternative educational choices. Chapter Ten provides tips and resources for parents. Chapter Eleven answers FAQs about homeschooling and the private school process. Chapter Twelve explains how we should rethink college and the options available to students.

There are many websites and books explaining the reasons for leaving public schools. There are lots of books about homeschooling, and some books provide tips for sending children to parochial or private schools. A few books provide information on how a church can start a school and how to navigate the regulations and legal requirements involved in alternative education.

This book encompasses all these areas and more. Whether you want to send your child to a private school, a faith-based school, start homeschooling, or join your local church in starting a school, this book provides a comprehensive guide to help you get started. There are plenty of alternatives available, but many parents are overwhelmed and unsure where to begin. Leaving the system takes a proactive resolve. It takes a well thought-out plan. It sometimes takes courage and almost always requires finances that many families don't think they have.

Parents who think they don't have the time, expertise, or money to educate their children outside of public schools are underestimating their abilities and the resources available. Take a deep breath, and then take one step at a time as you plan out a brighter future for your children.

Chapter One

Why Should You Leave Public Schools?

"Only those who live by faith really know what is happening in the world; the great masses without faith are unconscious of the destructive process going on, because they have lost the vision of the heights from which they have fallen."

Venerable Archbishop Fulton J. Sheen

In 2016, in Sevierville, Tennessee, three basketball players raped a freshman with a pool cue stick. The victim's bladder and colon ruptured, and the boy had to use a catheter and colostomy bag.

In 2018, an aide in a Charles County, Maryland school was sentenced to over 100 years in prison for sexually abusing dozens of teenagers and children. He was HIV positive at the time.

In February 2022, it was reported that over 75% of students at Baltimore City High School tested at the elementary level in reading and math.

In March 2022, in Pembroke Pines, Florida, a five-year-old student brutally beat a teacher to the point she needed to be hospitalized.

In January 2023, a six-year-old shot a first-grade teacher in the chest. He had previously said he hated her so much he wanted to set her on fire and watch her die.

Major Problems Plaguing Public Education

These incidents and statistics are just a few examples of what is occurring regularly in our public schools. An entire book could be written detailing just these types of problems as well as the increasingly dismal academic results. Most people never hear these stories because, although they are usually reported in the local news where they occur, national mainstream media will rarely report on them.

Besides academic failure and increasing levels of brutality and violence, many reasons have been given in recent years for leaving the public school system. A few include moral issues such as the sexualization of children, woke indoctrination, extreme propaganda, and limiting parental rights. These are all obviously valid reasons, but they certainly aren't the only ones. I have briefly outlined additional reasons why an increasing number of parents are taking their children out of government schools.

Public Schools Teach According to Birth Date, Not Ability

Most children will enter kindergarten when they are five years old. Having all kids begin school at the same age is a good place to start. It should not, however, remain this way until they graduate at age 18.

Imagine if every corporation and business in the United States issued a new policy regarding their employees. Starting immediately, everyone on staff will be grouped according to age. All staff members at age twenty-five will work in the mailroom until they are thirty. Those in their thirties will be in the accounting department, and forty-somethings will be in marketing. No one will work in upper management until at least age fifty. We don't care how hard you work, how many deals you make, or how successful you become. Employees are grouped by age and nothing else, and each will move along accordingly.

What business would ever do that and expect to succeed? How many people hoping to make the most of their talents and abilities would want to work for that company? Yet that is exactly what we do in our schools. It is called social promotion, and it is based on socialist and Marxist principles. It is an archaic method of herding kids from one grade to the next regardless of what they know or what they can do.

This method worked in spite of itself for many years because we didn't have all the other problems in public schools that we do now. However, continuing to educate children based on birth dates rather than performance and ability will only contribute to the further decline of public education, resulting in millions of students who never reach their academic potential while millions of others leave the system barely able to read, write, or do basic math. Social promotion is inefficient, illogical, and ultimately breeds mediocrity. Because of fear and political correctness, however, schools place social promotion and social agendas before actual education.

The result is that America is now dependent on individuals from foreign countries to fill many medical and technical positions because our own educational system has not produced enough students capable of entering high-level professions. They do not produce them because of social promotion and the expectation that all kids will do the same work at the same age. The solution is to move gifted kids and those with greater ability ahead more quickly.

Several years ago, I worked in a fourth-grade class with students who had the ability to do middle school work while others could barely read. Yes, teachers are adept at modifying plans and teaching to differing abilities. While teachers can manage these differences, it is often time-consuming and inefficient, especially when the differences are as vast as kindergarten and middle school.

Learning Is Standardized, Not Customized

Standardized learning is related to social promotion and the one-size-fits-all educational practices that too often occur in public education. When I taught in a large urban district, I distinctly remember that all teachers in each grade level had to maintain the same pace when teaching, especially in the reading and math curriculum. We all had to be in Unit 1, Chapter 1 during the same week. We all moved on to the next section, chapter, or unit together.

I understood why a large urban district did this. Many students were transitory and moved a lot, sometimes within the same school year. Wherever children moved within the district, the class they entered would often be on the same unit, chapter, etc., as the last school they attended. This provided continuity for children who often experienced instability in their lives. While this is understandable, there are ways to provide stability for these children while allowing other students to flourish and move ahead.

Most large school systems have several classes at each grade level within each school. At the district I worked in, there were usually three first-grade classes, three second-grade classes, and so forth. The ideal would have been to have an advanced class, an intermediate class, and a class for students struggling or below grade level.

This would benefit all students because they could more easily receive specialized instruction. Of course, that would not have been "politically correct" and even labeled racist. Social agendas and social justice are often put ahead of the basic academic needs of each student.

Private and parochial schools usually have smaller classes and greater autonomy regarding curriculum and what they choose to teach. This means education is often not as standardized as in most public schools. When my daughter was in a small parochial school that included kindergarten through 8th grade, her classes were sometimes small enough that the teachers could personalize lessons and areas of study for each student. This was particularly true in middle school when the students could often work independently.

Homeschooling obviously offers an even greater opportunity for personalization to occur. The curriculum and educational environment can be completely customized to each child.

Learning is Catered to the Lowest Common Denominator

This is a nice way of saying learning is dumbed-down. Both social promotion and standardized learning lead to lowered educational expectations. Teachers can't give each student the attention they need when classes are large, learning is taught by "the book" instead of customizing it to each child's needs, or a teacher is spending an inordinate amount of time attempting to maintain order in the classroom because of a handful of unruly students. Add to the equation political correctness, and we have a recipe for catering to the lowest common denominator.

The irony is that more students are on the honor roll in many schools than ever before. Children now receive A's and B's for mediocre work. Parents, families, and Americans in general now expect to receive the best in life, whether it is good grades, awards, or paychecks, for minimal effort.

It simplifies everything to make tests easy, hand out A's and B's, and just pass children on to the next grade even if they are not academically ready. Most teachers do not have the time or the energy to struggle against the parents or the system. When these things happen, which they do on a fairly regular basis, kids graduate from school without even the most basic academic skills and are often totally unprepared for real life.

Public Schools Lack Discipline and Are Increasingly Violent

Disciplining children, in or out of school, is nearly nonexistent in the current culture. When children grow up with little respect for authority and are accustomed to pretty much getting their own way, you end up with the chaotic society we now live in. Because of fears of lawsuits, many educators are truly terrified of promoting any type of discipline stern enough to discourage bad behavior.

While I do not encourage corporal punishment, one answer is to separate children with disciplinary issues. Remove them from the class. Period. This does not mean removing them from school, except in extreme circumstances. Keeping them in the same classroom, however, simply enables them to continue their bad behavior while at the same time holding back the rest of the class. Mollycoddling in public schools sets kids up for failure in adulthood. This is a big factor contributing to the school-to-prison pipeline.

In general, people will do whatever you allow them to do. This includes children. You often get in life whatever you are willing to put up with. It is not just incidents such as school shootings but fights between students, attacks on teachers, and bullying. Public schools routinely put up with behavior that has now become so unruly that many schools have metal detectors and constant police presence.

Parents Are Often Not Involved

Lack of parental participation is one of the starkest contrasts between public and private education. I saw this firsthand when working in public education while simultaneously sending my child to a parochial school. Parent involvement affects everything from discipline to keeping costs low. When too many parents see schools as a government entitlement, or worse, a babysitter, behavior is more difficult to manage, children often do not learn as well, and costs will inevitably rise.

Most people see the connection between well-behaved children and children who will learn more effectively because parents are involved, but reduced costs? Yes, dramatically reduced costs. The following are a few examples.

When kids have track meets, basketball games, etc., private and parochial schools often don't hire bus drivers. Instead, parents will take turns driving. The amount of money public schools spend on buses, drivers, and fuel is a huge cost. There also is not as much need for certain staffing positions when parents are involved and children have fewer disciplinary issues. In many schools, the primary job of vice principals and guidance counselors is what is sometimes called "conflict mediation." Their job basically revolves around resolving conflicts between students, which, in simplest terms, are disciplinary problems.

Public Schools Are Crowded

Classrooms with more than 15 or 20 students, especially at the elementary level, are simply too large. Classes with 25 to 30 students are not uncommon in a public school. Class size is normally quite a bit smaller in a private or parochial school. How many children each teacher is responsible for makes a crucial difference regarding how much one-on-one time the teacher can spend with each individual student. It also makes a difference in how well a teacher can manage students and handle discipline.

Children who are in overcrowded classrooms year after year during their entire educational experience will, over time, receive considerably less one-on-one instruction. From kindergarten through the senior year in high school, overcrowded classrooms and schools will make an enormous difference in educational outcomes.

Public Schools Spend Too Much Money

Yes, you read that correctly. The fact that parochial and private schools generally produce better results, often on a fraction of what public schools spend, proves that lack of money is not the root of the problems in public education. Big government entities, educational or otherwise, are notorious for throwing money at every problem. Bloated school bureaucracies and endless mandates used to social engineer society are not cheap. When most mandates are eliminated, only the most necessary administrators are hired, and parents contribute time and resources to the success of a school, costs are greatly reduced.

For those who still think schools need a lot of money, I will give you the ultimate example of why that's not true. In 1985, Judge Russell Clark decided that the Kansas City School District in Missouri should get all the money it wanted. They basically wanted to try an experiment to find out what would happen if money were absolutely no object and schools received all they wanted. And they did find out.

After receiving billions of dollars, the district built 15 new schools, dozens of magnet schools, programs for computer science, foreign languages, and classical Greek athletics. There was an Olympic-size swimming pool, a robotics lab, an art gallery, a planetarium, a film studio, a professional recording studio, and a zoo. There was not, however, any increase in student achievement.

This embarrassment is rarely talked about in public education circles, which is why most people today have never heard of it. But it proves that money is not the root of educational problems. All the money in the world does not address the foundational issues. Teaching solid academics, removing most of the non-academic social agendas, providing adequate discipline, and increasing parental involvement are some of the most basic factors in public education. Addressing these issues does not take a lot of money. It does take courage and dedication.

Public Schools Are Often Intrusive

Instead of just teaching skills, knowledge, and academics, schools have expanded their role and now intrude into areas once left to the families. Activists now use public schools to push their agendas on everything from nutritional programs, public safety issues, and mental health issues, to even moral issues. Not all of these mandates are bad or even controversial. One example is bicycle safety. Who would argue about teaching kids bicycle safety? But we simply do not have time for it when millions of kids leave the educational system uneducated.

The values taught in schools are often not the values parents hold. This is particularly true if you are a conservative Christian or generally adhere to traditional values. Traditional Christianity is usually either ignored or mocked as hateful and bigoted in public schools. Influences different from what your children learn at home can come from other students, teachers, and even the curriculum.

Why Reforming Schools Has Not Worked

People of differing beliefs and political stripes have attempted to reform the public school system for nearly 50 years. None of these efforts has proved to have any long-lasting effects. There are three general reasons why these efforts have failed and will continue to fail:

- **The Teachers' Unions** – Most teachers' unions, as the name implies, are good for the teachers, but generally not for the students. They are not called student unions for a reason. Whether teachers deserve higher pay or better benefits is not the issue. The fact is that teachers' unions have negotiated unsustainable salaries and benefits. Private and parochial teachers often make a fraction of public school pay and generally produce better results. These unions are also hyper-partisan, usually promoting a far-left agenda.

- **The Teachers' Colleges** – An entire book could be written regarding what is wrong with our current university system. At the end of this book, a short section explains how we can transform and improve universities. In short, colleges promote a far-left ideology, and students coming out of these colleges are increasingly promoting it in the classroom.

- **The Culture** – Schools and their surrounding communities are deeply interconnected. Let's be honest, many teachers face overwhelming difficulties managing behavior, coupled with unrealistic expectations. Schools, public or otherwise, are generally only as strong as the families that attend the school.

What happens in the public schools is directly related to the teachers' unions, the colleges that produce new teachers, and the culture that produces the types of families, parents, and parenting methods we currently have. Public education is a result of what occurs in these areas. You will never enact lasting, positive changes in public education unless there are lasting, positive changes in these three specific areas.

Past reform has normally involved training teachers, increasing teacher pay, changing curriculum, building new campuses, etc. These elements are all important but are only pieces of the puzzle. These things alone ultimately won't bring about lasting improvement.

In short, to see any real and lasting improvement in public education, there would need to be changes in these two major institutions as well as the culture. The irony is that the only way to really change the university system, the teachers' unions, and the culture is to raise and teach the next generation of children in a way that is profoundly different from how most children are raised and taught today.

Now that the case has been made to leave public education, what are the options?

Chapter Two

What Alternatives Are Available?

Several options are available for educating your child outside the public school system. The first thing to realize is that there isn't a one-size-fits-all solution for homeschooling, private education, or starting a school in your church. So parents are informed and understand each potential option available, I have included charter schools, which are closely tied to the public school system. The following are some of the educational choices available, what they normally involve, and the steps you can take to successfully participate.

1. Charter Schools

What Are Charter Schools?

Some people insist that charter schools are public schools, while others state that technically, they are not. These schools are publicly funded but operate independently. They are often started by community organizations, teachers, parents, and occasionally, for-profit groups. They sometimes receive a combination of tax money and private dollars but do not charge tuition.

They don't answer to the government or school boards but usually have to adhere to basic state curriculum requirements. I have included charter schools in the list because, basically, they are a hybrid approach, mixing elements of public and private education. This may work for some families. Charter school laws will vary from state to state. How much leeway the school will get regarding freedom to teach what they want will depend, in part, on the state the school is in.

In short, charter schools are on a leash held by the state. How long that leash is will depend on the state and how the founders put the school together.

How Do Charter Schools Work?

The "charter" lays out each school's goals, mission, and financial guidelines. The authorizer of the charter contract is sometimes a nonprofit, a university, a school district, or the state government. The authorizer may have the power to close down the charter school if it doesn't meet the contract terms. Approximately 7,000 charter schools are now in operation in North America.

Benefits can include the ability of teachers to think outside the box and implement innovative teaching methods. Charter schools normally have increased parental participation and a tight-knit community of families. The schools are free. One of the primary drawbacks is that charter schools can vary extensively in quality. There is sometimes a high turnover rate among teachers. Unfortunately, charter schools often close unexpectedly more often than other types of schools.

How Do You Get Into the Charter School of Your Choice?

Technically, charter schools can't deny any students who wish to attend. However, if more students apply than the school has room for, your child may be placed on a waitlist. The key to getting into the charter school of your choice is to apply early. A blind lottery may be held in cases where more students apply by the deadline than there are seats available.

What Are the Different Types of Charter Schools?

Sometimes charter schools are simply promoted as a general school, without any specialization or areas of particular interest. Other times, they have specialty areas. The following are a few examples.

- **Stem Charter Schools** – These schools might specialize in science and technology or have a detailed robotics program, computer programming classes, or other math specialties.

- **Language Immersion Schools** – Whether Spanish, French, or Chinese, children spend as much time learning and speaking another language as they do English.

- **Montessori** – Montessori is a popular method of learning in many charter schools. This method is explained in more detail later in this section.

Advantages

- Charter schools may have small classes and a community or family feeling among students and staff.

- Individual learning assistance and innovative teaching methods are often part of the charter school experience.

Disadvantages

- The quality of each school can vary widely. You may not know how good the school is until your child has been there for a while.

- These schools often operate on a shoestring budget. There may be a lot of fundraising requests and limits on school resources.

- There are sometimes high teacher turnover rates, and schools that are not run properly may get shut down.

2. Private/Parochial Schools

What Are Private and Parochial Schools?

Private schools are basically any type of school that is privately funded and operated. The government doesn't run or financially support a private school and doesn't have any say in how the school operates. Private education is a broad term that encompasses many types of education, including parochial or faith-based.

Parochial schools are specific types of private schools. The term "parochial" is often used loosely and might not mean the exact same thing in every area of the country. These schools are normally organized and supported by a particular church or denomination.

The primary difference between a religious school and a parochial school is that, by definition, a parochial school is usually directly connected to a specific church or Christian denomination. In general, a religious or faith-based school is not necessarily connected to a particular church or even Christianity.

How Do Private and Parochial Schools Work?

Contrary to what many people may believe, private schools are less discriminatory against minorities and low-income families than public schools. Unless a family can pay the housing prices and tax rate in a "good suburban" district, there is little chance their children will attend those schools. A private school, and especially parochial schools, will usually work with all types of families to help cover tuition costs. There are normally academic and need-based scholarships as well as other types of financial assistance available in most private schools.

How Do You Get Into the Private or Parochial School of Your Choice?

Getting into a private or parochial school can be more difficult than most other types of schooling choices. If possible, you will want to start doing your research and looking into different schools at least a year or more before you want your child to start. Make sure you choose a school that is a good fit for your child and your entire family. As appealing as it may sound, do not go to a school just because a family member is sending a child there or your child's best friend is going there.

To be brutally honest, the cost is normally not what keeps families out of parochial and other faith-based schools. Lack of commitment and involvement on the part of the parents and discipline issues with the child will more likely keep a family from these types of schools. Most schools are willing to work with families based on their income.

While most faith-based schools will accept students regardless of their personal beliefs or church affiliation, this will be an important aspect of the educational process. For example, if your family is Baptist and your child is attending a Catholic school, your child will almost certainly be taught doctrines and be expected to participate in activities related to Catholic Church teachings.

What Are the Different Types of Private and Parochial Schools?

There are several different types of private and parochial choices available.

- **Standard Private Schools** – A private school is any type of school or educational system that is not part of and does not have to adhere to the public schools. All the following schools would fall in the category of private schools.

- **Faith-Based or Religious Private Schools** – This is a type of private school that is faith-based, and normally associated with a certain religious belief. It could be Christian or another religion.

- **Parochial Private Schools** – A parochial school is specifically associated with a particular church or Christian denomination. A school can be faith-based, but not associated with a specific church. In short, all parochial schools are normally faith-based, but all faith-based schools are not parochial.

- **Boarding Private Schools** – Boarding schools are private institutions where students actually live full-time or at least part-time.

According to the National Center for Education Statistics, approximately 10 percent of all students in elementary and secondary schools were educated in private schools in 2015. Since that time, and particularly since the pandemic, that number has almost certainly risen.

Most private schools are Catholic. About 60 percent of Catholic schools are parochial and are associated with a particular church or diocese. Some still provide religious education but are independent of any individual church. These schools are faith-based but not considered parochial.

Besides Catholic schools, other parochial schools include Lutheran (primarily Missouri Synod), Baptist, Episcopal, Presbyterian, and non-denominational. There are also hundreds of Jewish schools throughout the United States.

Advantages

- Private, parochial, and faith-based schools almost always have smaller classes, and teachers can spend more one-on-one time with each student.

- There is often a strong sense of community among families and students in these types of schools.

- There is almost always less violence and less exposure to curriculum and peer influence that parents may see as inappropriate.

- Values and religious beliefs of the parents will usually be reinforced in parochial and faith-based schools.

- In general, students have higher test scores, graduate from high school at higher rates, and are more likely to attend and finish college after attending these types of schools.

Disadvantages

- While many private, parochial, and faith-based schools will work with families financially, it still can be costly for children to attend.

- There may be fewer choices regarding courses, extracurricular activities, and athletics.

- Some teachers may not have as much training or education.

- There may not be special education classes available.

3. Homeschools

What Are Homeschools?

The most basic definition of a homeschool is parents or caregivers educating children outside of public or private school, usually in a home environment. The education process, however, can take place throughout the community, with other families, or online. Homeschooling is truly a type of education that could involve a variety of locations, experiences, and people.

One of the great things about homeschooling is that you do not have to worry about getting into the school of your choice. You can create your own school that fits the specific needs of your children. It is important to note that there is almost an infinite number of ways "to do homeschooling."

How Do Homeschools Work?

Homeschooling is usually parent-directed education that takes place at home. Beyond that, there really is not a one-size-fits-all definition for homeschooling. With this in mind, how it works is pretty open-ended. There are several different styles and methods of homeschooling. It can be structured, with a daily schedule for each subject that a family pretty much sticks to, or it can look like what might be referred to as "free range" education.

How Do You Start a Homeschool?

Each homeschool is as unique as the children you are educating. The question of how to start a homeschool is answered in detail in the next chapter.

What Are the Different Types of Homeschools?

There are as many types of homeschools as there are families that embark on the journey to find their own educational path. There are, however, several models and methods that you can use as guidelines when creating the right homeschool for your children. The following information describes different types of homeschools.

Traditional Homeschooling

This is sometimes called "school" at home because it uses much of the same set-up and structure as both public and private schooling. Traditional homeschooling might include a similar daily schedule and learning timetable as a regular school. The traditional school-at-home method might be taught by a parent, a group of parents, or facilitated by an online instructor.

Advantages

- This method provides predictable schedules and lots of curriculum options since the curriculum is often similar to what is found in public schools.

- It can be used as a transition method from the public schools until a family decides what other method they want to use.

- You will know exactly where your child is as far as grade level and what material the child's peers are covering.

Disadvantages

- While almost any curriculum can be adapted, if parents are unhappy with the public school curriculum, this may not be a good choice.

- Following too structured a routine may not leave time for creative learning, field trips, or other hands-on activities.

- It may be stressful for parents to maintain a rigid schedule on a daily basis.

Classical

This is a style of learning that came from both the ancient Romans and Greeks. This method consists of separate stages of learning within what is called the *Trivium* and the *Quadrivium*. The Trivium consists of Phase 1, or the *Grammar Stage,* which focuses on learning basic information that will form the building blocks for more advanced learning. This includes absorbing and memorizing the rules of phonics, spelling, and grammar. It also involves learning multiplication tables and basic science facts. Phase 2, the *Logic or Dialectic Stage*, consists of teaching understanding. Phase 3, the *Rhetoric Stage*, teaches wisdom.

The Quadrivium consists of four subjects. These include arithmetic, geometry, astronomy, and music. The Quadrivium is generally taught after the Trivium. Theology, particularly for Christians, permeates all areas of both the Trivium and the Quadrivium.

There is also a Biblical Classical approach that includes Hebrew concepts from the Old Testament. This method could incorporate an emphasis on Greek and Latin, as well as intense biblical studies.

Advantages

- There is a major emphasis on reading, and students will explore lots of great books from different cultures.

- There is also an emphasis on different languages. These often include Greek, Latin, Spanish, French, and German.

- Logical and critical thinking, which is often neglected in public and even many private schools, is a big part of Classical Education.

- This method provides rigor and is time-tested. Classical Education has been in use for thousands of years.

- Because Classical Education has been around for a long time, there are lots of materials and networking options available.

Disadvantages

- Some families may find the reading requirements overwhelming, particularly if a student struggles with any reading disabilities.

- Some people may find the Classical method less adaptable or flexible than some of the other homeschool methods.

- Parents may believe learning Greek and Latin to be impractical. Others, however, see it as providing a solid educational background.

Charlotte Mason

This method views education more as an atmosphere or a way of life than as passing tests or training for a job. There is an emphasis on great literature, poetry, art, and music. Biblical knowledge is an important aspect of this type of education. Science emphasizes hands-on nature study. The method also involves aspects of Classical Education and Unit

Studies. There are lots of curriculum options available that are based on the Charlotte Mason method.

Advantages

- Learning is hands-on with activities such as nature walks and lots of journaling.

- This is considered a low-cost option in comparison to many other methods.

- It is not as old as Classical but has been around for more than 100 years.

- Charlotte Mason is Christian-based and may be a good option for those seeking a biblical education method.

Disadvantages

- The method is primarily elementary age-oriented. It is not as strong at the middle or high school level.

- The method does not have a strong emphasis on math, science, or modern technology.

Montessori

Physician Maria Montessori developed the Montessori method in the early 20th century. This method deviates from formal instructional methods and puts a focus on individual learning. It includes mixed ages in classrooms. While it can be modified to meet a family's individual needs, Montessori is generally considered a secular educational method. However, this method, like most others, can be adapted to be compatible with Christianity.

Advantages

- This method promotes individual needs since children are pretty much allowed to work at their own pace. It is also considered special needs friendly.

- Montessori emphasizes creativity and the arts.

- It is very adaptable and enables a lot of self-directed learning.

Disadvantages

- There aren't a lot of families that use the Montessori method. This means there will be fewer networking options and resources available.

- The method is primarily for younger children and is normally not used for middle or high school students.

- It is based on a humanist, secular ideology. Parents with faith-based values may not want to use this method.

Unit Studies

This is a method that is based on studying various themes. You will choose a theme each week, every two weeks, or monthly, and then each subject revolves around that particular theme. For example, if children are studying the ocean, then each subject, including reading, writing, history, science, and math, will all have something to do with ocean study. You might take a field trip to an aquarium or start a project involving a home aquarium. Children could read a book about the ocean and then write an essay. They might work on a project regarding the history of ocean research and important individuals in this field for social studies and history. Math might include something as simple as counting fish for younger students. This provides a practical way to study since subjects will often overlap.

Advantages

- Unit Studies can easily be incorporated into almost any other method of home-schooling, including Classical and Charlotte Mason. This means an abundance of materials and networking options will likely be available.

- This method promotes a holistic approach to learning. Most subjects are not isolated and often overlap.

- Weaker subjects for students may improve since they are often interconnected with stronger subjects.

- Students may consider this one of the more fun homeschooling methods since it often includes a lot of field trips, games, and hands-on activities.

Disadvantages

- Unit Studies is technically not a philosophy or an official approach to education. There is not a "big picture" to this method.

- Since there isn't a universal model, the method can be very curriculum-dependent and is often better when connected to another method or approach.

- Since subjects are all interconnected, some subjects may not get enough attention, and students may suffer from "gaps of knowledge."

Waldorf

Austrian educator Rudolph Steiner started the Waldorf Method in Germany in 1919. The Waldorf method puts an emphasis on imagination, and in particular, the arts and nature. Students might spend a lot of time working on artistic projects or outside exploring nature. Music, dance, and literature are the primary focuses of the method, with a big emphasis on a child's imagination.

Advantages

- For those interested in the creative arts, Waldorf is a method that focuses on artistic endeavors.

- Learning occurs at a slower, more natural pace. In the earlier years, there aren't computers, tablets, or even calculators.

Disadvantages

- Some of the advantages may be disadvantages for other families. For example, the slow learning pace may not be ideal for some students.

- While sometimes disconnecting from technology is good for learning, not using technology until almost middle school may be counterproductive.

- Waldorf is based on a philosophy known as anthroposophy. Some adherents claim it is compatible with Christianity, but there are many serious contradictions between traditional Christianity and anthroposophy. Parents raising their children in doctrinally correct Christianity will not want to use this method.

Unschooling

Unschooling is a bit controversial, but it may work for some children. This involves letting kids follow a very loose structure and centers around a child's interests. There isn't any real schedule to keep or curriculum to follow. Children study and learn what they are interested in. Kids are generally never forced to learn anything. People who use this method often prioritize family and personal relationships over the expectations of society. The following are some methods and ways to put together an unschooling experience. These can also be incorporated into other types of learning methods as well.

- **Eclectic** – This involves mixing and matching a variety of learning methods to put together a highly individual teaching routine for each child. Although the term "eclectic" is not heard much, this is often what a lot of parents who homeschool end up doing, whether they intentionally mean to or not.

- **Multiple Intelligence** – This is a method that focuses on each student's learning style. For example, if a child is primarily a visual learner, reading would be taught with an emphasis on learning sight words with less time spent on phonics.

- **Free Range** – Free range is sometimes called self-directed or unschooling. Kids who are educated using this method may never follow a lesson plan, take a test, or even receive an actual grade. School is not broken down into subjects and time frames. Parents see themselves not so much as teachers but as facilitators. This may work well with children who are self-motivated and disciplined, especially older children. However, if a child is not learning basic reading, writing, and math skills after a reasonable amount of time, parents will need to take a more hands-on approach.

Advantages

- Unschooling is very adaptable and completely revolves around individual students and their learning needs.

- This type of education allows students to pursue their passions, which means children will likely be more interested in learning.

- This method promotes diversity and allows parents to be as involved or hands-off as they want to be.

Disadvantages

- This method lacks structure and may be unsuitable for students who aren't organized and self-motivated.

- Since children learn what they want, when they want, there may be many skills and basics they may not learn.

- Even many homeschoolers often frown on this type of method. Therefore, it may be difficult to find a lot of networking options.

- There may be challenges in meeting testing and other legal requirements in some states.

4. Umbrella Schools

What Are Umbrella Schools?

Like many other types of schools, there is a loose definition for the term umbrella school, and what it exactly looks like can vary. Umbrella schools are usually private schools that provide an option for homeschoolers. They help homeschool families by overseeing the educational process and helping them meet their state's legal requirements. Some states have very few requirements for homeschooling. Other states, however, have more stringent requirements. In these states, it may be beneficial to become part of an umbrella school to make sure you meet all legal requirements.

How Do Umbrella Schools Work?

Umbrella schools normally provide some level of legal protection as well as academic support for students in the school. This will vary from state to state. Specific things an umbrella school might provide for students include attendance records, report cards, and hosting academic clubs and field trips. An umbrella school can provide legitimacy for a family's homeschool program. This may be especially important in a state that has a lot of testing, curriculum, attendance, and other requirements for homeschoolers.

How Do You Get Into an Umbrella School?

Since there are different types of umbrella schools, standards for getting in will vary. Many private schools, in particular Christian schools, will offer umbrella programs for homeschooled families. The requirements for getting into the umbrella program may be the same as for the regular school. In other cases, there may be different or less stringent requirements. While the fees will likely not be as high as the cost to regularly attend the school, there will be some costs involved.

What Are the Different Types of Umbrella Schools?

There are private (secular) umbrella schools and parochial or faith-based schools of this type. These are generally the only type of umbrella schools. Umbrella schools are as diverse as private and parochial schools can be. Some states, such as Florida, Tennessee, and Maryland, have quite a few umbrella schools. Other states, such as Texas and Indiana, may have very limited options regarding umbrella schools.

Advantages

- Families will have access to the expertise and services that umbrella schools provide.

- The school will likely offer networking opportunities with other homeschooling families.

Disadvantages

- Some umbrella schools may require that a family use a certain curriculum.

- In some cases, families may be required to attend a certain church or sign faith statements.

5. Co-ops

What Are Co-ops?

Another option within the realm of homeschooling is joining or putting together a co-op. A homeschool co-op is several homeschool families getting together to share resources and the responsibilities of teaching. Co-ops can have only a few families or several. They might only get together occasionally for field trips or special projects. Other times they are together regularly, taking turns teaching each other's children different subjects. Co-ops might include only a few families that get together a few times each month or large organizations with dozens of families. Co-ops are as individual and flexible as the people who put them together.

How Do Co-ops Work?

Each of the families in the co-op will need to sit down and agree on a detailed plan of how their co-op will work. How often will you meet? Once a week for one subject? Or will you meet daily and take turns teaching different subjects? What is expected of each family and child, and how many families and children will be allowed in the co-op must be established early on and agreed on by every member. If you join a co-op that is already established, you will want to get to know some of the families and understand explicitly what is expected before joining the group.

How Do You Get Into a Co-op?

Start by talking to other homeschool families in your church or local community about co-op options. If you are new to homeschooling, you can start by searching the words "homeschool," "homeschoolers," or "co-op" and the name of your town or nearby towns online.

What Are the Different Types of Co-ops?

The following are a few co-op examples:

1. Three families with children in the middle school age range plan to meet at a local library for a few hours on Tuesday and Thursday afternoons for math classes. One parent who has a background in math agrees to teach the class in exchange for either payment or the other parents offering to provide their own teaching, activities, etc. for the kids.

2. Over a dozen families with children of varying ages have pooled their money to hire a teacher who provides online instruction or they have paid for online courses in various subjects. The students take the classes and receive instruction in their own homes. The students then get together once a week to work on and discuss material from the classes.

3. A group of families gets together occasionally, primarily for social interaction. Activities may include field trips and playdates. Parents take turns planning and supervising each activity.

Advantages

- Co-ops usually provide a high level of accountability. When you are working with several other adults and you are responsible for teaching other children, it is extremely difficult to miss lessons or skip entire days without being held accountable. When it is just your family homeschooling alone, it is much easier to slack off.

- Co-ops can provide solutions for difficult subjects such as math, science, or foreign language instruction, especially when children are in older grades.

- Even if you are only in a casual co-op that meets a few times a month, you will have a support system and a network of resources.

- Co-ops will provide increased social interaction and a wider circle of friends for your children.

Disadvantages

- Conflicts and disagreements may more easily occur. The more families that are part of a co-op, the greater the chance for disagreements regarding everything from discipline to teaching methods used.

- Laws regarding co-ops will vary from state to state. Some areas, such as Washington, D.C., currently have laws stating that no one but a parent or guardian is allowed to homeschool a child. There may be laws regarding how many children are allowed in a co-op.

- Larger co-ops with more families can have classes as large as those in public schools. This means each child will not receive as much individual attention, and disciplinary issues may arise.

- Some co-op groups may claim to be educational but are really no more than daycare for kids. You will want to thoroughly research any co-op that you don't personally start or oversee.

- Unfortunately, cliques can occur among both students and parents in co-ops.

6. Boarding Schools

What Are Boarding Schools?

Do boarding schools still exist? And are there any for students in the United States? Yes, and yes. There aren't that many, however, and most are on the East Coast. They are primarily for children who are old enough for middle and high school. A boarding school is technically any type of educational organization in which a child stays in a residential setting while learning. There are approximately 300 boarding schools in the United States, with at least a few in nearly every state. Many are faith-based, while others are military-style schools.

How Do Boarding Schools Work?

There are several reasons parents may choose to send a child to a boarding school. These include that some boarding schools have innovative and unique educational programs, such as an emphasis on STEM classes. A boarding school might have ice rinks, equestrian centers, and crew teams. They may also give a child an edge when getting into the college of his or her choice. Some parents may want their children to live more independently before the age of 18.

How Do You Get Into the Boarding School of Your Choice?

The costs for boarding schools are comparable to what a parent would pay for private college. Acceptance rates vary as well. Some can be difficult to get into, with acceptance rates as low as 30 percent. Since most boarding schools are for middle and high school students, elementary school will be the time to make sure children have the background that will make them eligible for the boarding school of their choice.

Extracurricular activities and achievements in music, the arts, and athletics will be important. You will also want to make sure your child has volunteer experience in your community. While grades are important, having a well-rounded life experience is normally more essential in the admission process for a boarding school.

Advantages

- One of the primary reasons to send a child to a boarding school is to improve their chances of getting into a good college.

- Students will already be socializing with peers who will likely be attending college as well. They will be making strong social connections earlier in life.

- Boarding schools provide excellent academic opportunities, extracurricular, athletics, and social activities all in one place.

Disadvantages

- It may not be the best choice for children to be away from family for extensive periods at a younger age.

- Parents will not have a direct influence on much of their child's upbringing.

- There may be excessive pressure for a child to succeed.

- Boarding schools are often very expensive.

7. Virtual/Online Schools

What Are Virtual/Online Schools?

Online learning is generally defined as any internet portal or site that features instruction or educational content. There are both public school online options and those that are private. After typing in "types of online education for students," you will find lots of articles and blogs providing information about various online education, as well as actual schools and platforms to choose from.

Online schooling is quickly gaining in popularity. According to some statistics, close to 400,000 K through 12 students are engaged in virtual or online schooling. While parents do not have to be instructors, such as when they are homeschooling, they will need to be more involved than in other types of schooling to make an online education successful.

How Do Virtual/Online Schools Work?

These platforms are also called e-learning. Some are official schools, other types are membership-based, and some are free. There are dozens, if not hundreds, of online learning platforms, schools, and educational systems to choose from.

Online school teachers will communicate with parents and students through web conferencing, email, and phone. Students may watch live instruction or download previously recorded instruction. They will read a lot of online and downloaded material and send assignments through online portals and websites.

Just like most anything else that is on the internet, there are dangers to watch out for and precautions to take. Since almost anyone can start an online school, educational program, or offer courses on the Internet, the quality of some may be questionable. Anyone can throw up a blog, a website, a video, etc., and teach classes. If it is not a well-known school or educational program, you will want to do some research about the site.

Since many online schools are public and free, parents may decide to try this before paying for a private or parochial online school. Even if it is public, you will eliminate a lot of the problems connected to public schools by educating your child at home online. Large class sizes, discipline problems, and exposure to violence and negative peer influence will primarily be eliminated. (There may still be some peer influence, as some programs will allow various degrees of interaction online.) The curriculum, however, may not be what you want your child to be taught. If you choose this route, you will need to closely monitor what is taught and what happens while your child is online.

How Do You Start Online Schooling?

The first step is to make sure you have all the necessary equipment. You will want to invest in at least two computers, preferably a laptop and a desktop computer. It is important to have two computers in case one breaks down and needs repairing. You will also need a printer. Making sure you have two good computers, one always connected to a printer and one that is portable, is essential. You will probably also need a webcam. A desk, chairs, and a work table will need to be set up in an area that is designated for school and study.

A total online education is probably not the best approach because a child needs face-to-face social interaction as well as hands-on activities. This is true no matter what the age of the child. Online instruction, however, will almost certainly be at least part of the educational process no matter what type of schooling children have. If online or virtual instruction is your primary method of choice, you will want to implement a hybrid method that involves, at least occasionally, other types of experiences. The following information explains some examples of how to mix different types of educational methods with online education.

What Are the Different Types of Online Schools?

The following are a few of the different types of online school options.

Full-time Online Education: There are many types of full-time options available for students of all ages. Even if you select a full-time online program, you will want to make sure your child engages in plenty of face-to-face and hands-on extracurricular and social activities.

Hybrid Approach: Some online learning may be in real time, while other classes students can complete on their own time. Different types of online learning may also be combined with in-person learning in an actual school. For example, a student may attend two or three high school classes in the morning and then take the rest of their classes online in the afternoon. A home school family might use the Charlotte Mason Method three days each week and use online learning two days a week while parents work from home.

Supplemental Online Education: The difference between a supplemental and hybrid approach is that when you are supplementing, this normally only involves one or two online classes or what would amount to a few hours a week online. Hybrid would likely involve more time spent in online learning. Supplementing another program or method with online classes is an excellent way to make sure your child receives a well-rounded educational experience.

Synchronous Online Classes: These classes take place in real-time and require students to all be online at the same time. This is similar to interacting on a webinar.

Asynchronous Classes: Students can watch instructional videos and other content and then complete assignments within a certain time. Interaction with instructors or other students may take place on discussion boards, emails, or blogs.

Interactive Online Learning: This is where educators and learners can communicate in real-time with one another interactively, like Zoom. In fact, Zoom, as well as many other similar types of interactive platforms, can be used for educational purposes.

There are now so many online school programs and courses available that it would take a whole book just to list and explain the different companies and individuals providing online education and how each works.

Some online programs are independently run, while others are associated with or part of established brick-and-mortar schools. Some are tuition-free and run by local public schools, while others are part of private institutions. Most, especially at the elementary level, will require quite a bit of parental supervision and oversight.

You will want to research if the online program or school you are interested in has licensed teachers for either live virtual classes or pre-recorded classes. Some programs, in addition to academic instruction, may provide social and extracurricular wrap-around services.

Advantages

- Much of the online school curriculum is already organized and set up. A daily and weekly schedule for learning is already in place.

- There are affordable and even free online educational choices available. In co-ops, families may go together to purchase an online class or program.

- Most programs will provide lots of teacher support and peer interaction. Some programs may offer 24/7 support and interaction.

Disadvantages

- Unless your online learning program includes hybrid or supplemental learning, students may miss out on a lot of hands-on activities and social interaction.

- Online learning is sometimes less flexible. Some programs allow students to log on and watch at any time, while others require students to watch only at a certain time.

- Some children already spend too much time online, making more screen time a problem. It is also easier to "take shortcuts" to learning since children can easily look things up online.

8. Waldorf Schools

Waldorf was mentioned under the homeschool section since parents can use this philosophy when putting together a homeschool program for their children. It is, however, also a specific type of school, with approximately 130 schools in the United States and 1200 worldwide.

In a nutshell, Waldorf schools are about doing and experiencing subjects, not reading or primarily engaging in bookwork and then taking tests about subjects. There is an emphasis on music, art, dancing, and theater. Most Waldorf schools are private, although this philosophy has been incorporated into some public schools. Humanitarian principles and social justice are emphasized. Looping is often encouraged, which means a child remains with the same teacher for several years in a row.

Rudolph Steiner started the Waldorf schools, opening the first school in 1919. It is important to note that Steiner based his educational model on what is known as anthroposophy. This is a spiritual philosophy, and some might even consider it a religion. This belief subscribes to spirits on the earth and a belief in reincarnation. This has a strong connection to New Age ideas. Christian parents would obviously have concerns about sending their child to a school that even indirectly promotes these ideas and beliefs.

9. Hybrid Approach

What Are Hybrid Approaches?

A hybrid approach is a mixture of one or more of the previous types of educational choices. This is also called a blended approach. Sometimes it is a mix of several methods. Some of the previous choices would more likely work better together than others. Online education is one method that can be incorporated with almost any other method to form a hybrid approach.

There are online schools that also offer a blended method. They provide online classes and curriculum, and generally conduct most work online, but also offer occasional on-site classes for students. Some online academies have what are called "drop-by" or "drop-in" centers. Students can stop by to participate in extracurricular activities, receive tutoring, or spend time socializing with other students who are part of the online school.

How Do Hybrid Educational Methods Work?

One example of a hybrid method would include incorporating Unit Studies into a Classical Education. Another example would be using parts of Charlotte Mason's methods in a traditional homeschool approach. You might also use any of the methods as part of unschooling, making it a bit more structured. The different combinations and how much you would use of each method when combining them are almost endless.

If you are using some form of online education with another method, you will want to try different ratios of time spent online and time off. A good place to start is 80 percent offline and 20 percent online. An online approach can be part of basically every other alternative schooling method available. A certain amount of online education probably should be incorporated into whatever method you choose. In our current society, so much of most people's lives are spent online that it is important that children learn how to work and thrive on the internet and how to create a healthy balance between time spent online and off.

What Are Some Different Options When Putting Together Hybrid Learning?

There are endless ways you can put together a hybrid educational process. The following are a few ideas.

- **Pods** – This is a relatively new concept that basically started during COVID-19. A pod is normally a small group of students in the same general age range. They have left the public or even private school setting. A licensed teacher may be hired to teach one or more subjects.

- **Cottage Schools** – These are technically private schools. They are sometimes run by parents, similar to a co-op but more formal. Sometimes, teachers or groups of investors may start a cottage school. It is normally a very small school.

- **Enrichment Centers** – These are similar to cottage schools but may just be for a specific subject or activity. As the name suggests, this is enrichment, not an overall school.

- **Microschools** – Microschools are small private schools that have been formed by a parent or a group of parents. Sometimes, a group of teachers might organize the school. This may be similar to a cottage school.

- **Independent Study Program** – This is sometimes offered by the local public school district and possibly by a private or parochial school.

- **Independent Study Course** – This is like the above program, but is a single course.

Advantages

- A hybrid approach would offer the most flexibility of all homeschool and private options. You could easily personalize education to fit the individual needs of your children and family.

- Parents would be able to support the diverse learning styles of each child. This would work well for a child with learning disabilities and special needs.

- Since there usually is not a set curriculum or timetable to follow, it is easier to incorporate extracurricular and social activities.

Disadvantages

- Putting together an effective hybrid program would take a lot of time and effort. There would not be just one specific curriculum to follow, and parents would have to organize and put together material and lesson plans for subjects not covered by a school or professional instructor.

- Unless you are very organized and have set goals and a timetable to meet those goals, it can be easy to fall behind regarding certain skills or being ready to take and meet state testing standards.

Each of these methods can be tweaked and modified to fit each family's specific needs. Most homeschoolers probably do not exclusively follow one method directly, but incorporate different methods, styles, and curricula into their homeschooling system.

It may be easier to start off following a particular method, but once you get the hang of homeschooling, you will be able to modify and adjust, add and take away, until you find the type of educational system that fits your needs. No two homeschools are going to look exactly alike.

General Tips for Succeeding in All Types of Educational Settings

No matter what type of school you are hoping to get your child into or start, there are some general tips and guidelines you will want to keep in mind.

Gather Important Transcripts and Records – You will need to get all transcripts together from any school your child has previously attended. Transcripts would include records of all grades and classes completed, attendance records, and extracurricular records. Even if you are going to homeschool, you will want to keep track of all records about your child's education. Teacher and coach recommendations would also be helpful if you are trying to get into a private school. Finally, get copies from your healthcare provider of all vaccinations and important medical records for your child. It is crucial to keep all these records up-to-date and organized.

Checklist for transcripts and records. (Write each child's name and the date records are obtained in the following spaces.)

Grades and Classes Completed

Attendance Records

Extracurricular Records

Vaccination/Medical Records

Keep Track of Deadlines – All schools have deadlines for different stages of the application process. There are forms to fill out, medical records to send in, and meetings and orientations to attend. Missing important deadlines may not only make it more difficult for your child to be accepted but can also get you off on the wrong foot with teachers and administrators.

Get Your Child Involved – While parents are ultimately in charge of making decisions for their children, each child should be able to speak for him or herself during any meetings or interviews. Children should also help prepare application essay questions, if possible, and tour the facility with the parents.

Take Tours – Take tours of different schools, even of the schools you probably will not send your child to attend. The reason for this is to get a broad understanding of the different schools and educational programs that are available and be able to compare each of them. If you are considering joining a homeschool co-op, ask if your child could have a trial period attending a few of the classes to find out if it would be a good fit.

Ace Interviews and Applications – For interviews, you want to look professional but not stiff. Nice jeans and a blazer are a good choice. Be prepared to answer questions such as why you want to go to a particular school, why you want to leave your current school, and your parenting style. Also, be able to describe your child's personality. Take your time when filling out applications. It is a good idea to set aside an application for a few days after you finish filling it out. Go back and reread your application and decide if you need to make any changes.

Chapter Three

How Can You Start a Homeschool or a Co-op?

I f you have decided to homeschool at home, with a co-op, or perhaps using your church building, there are several steps you will need to take to get the process started.

As this book is written, homeschooling is legal in all 50 states. Laws and regulations regarding homeschooling in each state are different and sometimes change. Keeping up-to-date on laws and various changes is one of the first and most important things you will need to do as a homeschool parent.

There are several aspects of homeschooling you will need to make decisions about before getting started. The good thing about homeschooling that is a little different from most other educational choices is that homeschooling provides more flexibility. You can easily change your mind if something is not working out.

Making Decisions

Who is officially in charge and how to conduct general communication needs to be decided early in the process, especially if you are putting together a co-op. Even two parents homeschooling a few children need to have predetermined guidelines in place regarding who will make decisions about selecting curriculum, how to discipline, hours of daily instruction time, etc.

Undertaking the enormous task of homeschooling will almost certainly affect a marriage. Like many other things in life, it will bring some couples closer together while driving a wedge between others. Whether you are working with friends, family, or a spouse, it is important to keep your relationships a priority when starting the homeschooling process. Deciding ahead of time who is in charge, when and how you will discipline, what type of curriculum you will use, and what schedule you will adhere to will go a long way in easing stress levels.

Person Primarily in Charge

Discipline Methods

Curriculum Choices

Schedule Options

Choosing a Location

For most people who choose to homeschool, the location will be obvious. However, you will need to decide which rooms or areas of the home you will primarily use for learning. Just as people who work from home need a designated space with necessary technology tools and other materials, children need a specific space as well. You may want to use a spare bedroom, a den, or part of a finished basement. Even if you are unschooling, there should be a "headquarters," per se, where students can gather to start the day or make general decisions.

Area of the House for Homeschooling

Furniture Needed

Setting Rules & Structure

If you are homeschooling, how many days each week will kids receive instruction? How many hours each day? Will you teach each subject every day or will some subjects like spelling and science be taught only a few times each week? These are just a few questions you need to answer. What type of discipline will you use? Each adult involved in the homeschooling process will need to be on the same page regarding the general rules and guidelines.

Days to Homeschool

Time / Hours for Homeschooling

Subjects to Teach

Days Each Subject is Taught

Understanding Legal Requirements

There are specific legal requirements for homeschooling in each state. Chapter Six explains this in more detail.

Creating a Budget

Tips for saving money and setting up a budget are explained in more detail in Chapters Eight and Nine. There are also other steps you can take to help defray costs. One is to apply for grants. There are grants available not only for public schools, private and parochial schools but for homeschoolers as well. In particular, there are curriculum grants available. These grants are often worth a few hundred dollars per child, and there are requirements to qualify.

Teaching

Who will do all or most of the teaching? Will you be part of a co-op where different parents teach different subjects? Will you hire an online instructor to teach certain subjects? If homeschooling, you'll need to decide if you will personally teach all subjects, join a co-op, hire an instructor, or put together a hybrid approach.

Who Will Do the Teaching?

Selecting a Method, Curriculum, and Instruction Style

The different methods for homeschool instruction are discussed in Chapter Two. Will you use the Charlotte Mason Method, the Classical Method, or another type of instruction? Many families end up using a hybrid approach that incorporates different elements of several methods and instruction styles. Some parents may use one method for language arts instruction and another for math and science.

While choosing an instructional method is one of the bigger decisions you will need to make, it is also important to remember that you can adjust, modify, and even scrap a method if it is just not working for your children. This is one reason it is recommended to invest in a minimal amount of curriculum materials, or at least buy used ones until you have tried a method for a few months and know if you like it.

If you spend a lot on a curriculum package and discover it is just not working for you, don't tough it out. If you are frustrated and your children are struggling academically, there are other options besides trying to struggle through a curriculum that is not working. You should be able to resell the curriculum online or through homeschool groups.

Curriculums can be expensive. Until you have tried something and are sure it is the right fit for your students, you may want to try to borrow or buy used.

List Possible Curriculum Choices

Gathering Supplies

Once you have decided where the primary location for learning will take place and what type of curriculum or method you'll start with, you will want to start thinking about supplies. This will start with furniture. Will your kids sit at a desk or a table, or will you create a more casual atmosphere? Most students need a desk or table for at least part of their learning time.

The list of smaller supplies you will need is almost endless. A few examples include the following: puzzles, blocks, pens, pencils, crayons, markers, paints, paintbrushes, butcher paper, felt boards, scissors, glitter, glue, sponges, modeling clay, colored pipe cleaners, books of varying sizes and reading levels, and baskets full of dress-up clothes.

Use old tin cans, Mason jars, baby food jars, and even containers made from painted popsicle sticks to store smaller supplies. Besides shelves, use laundry baskets and stackable crates for large items. Use tote bags and over-the-chair storage pockets for notebooks and other schoolwork. Hang up a clothesline for drying art projects and use bulletin boards for displaying written work.

What Supplies Are Needed?

Making Educational Plans

An educational plan for a student is similar to an Individualized Education Plan (IEP) for special needs students in public schools or an Individualized Service Plan (ISP) in private schools. If possible, every child should have an individualized plan stating their educational goals and the detailed steps for reaching them whether they are in a private school, a homeschool setting, or a co-op.

Goals should be based on academic skills that a child should learn at approximately each age or grade level. These skills are listed in Chapter Seven of this book. For example, a large goal might be for a child to learn the multiplication table 0 through 10 by the end of third grade or age 9. This could be broken down further by having the child learn 0 through 5 in the first semester and the rest during the second semester. Weekly or monthly goals might include learning multiplication by 2s in September and 3s in October.

Another goal could include a child increasing her reading wpm (words per minute) rate by 10 points by the end of the semester. Other goals might include finishing a geography project by the end of the week or visiting two museums by the end of the month.

Whatever goals you make, they need to be measurable and specific. For example, *becoming a better reader* is vague, while *reading 130 wpm by the end of the semester* is specific and measurable. *Understanding geometry concepts* is vague, while *being able to successfully complete perimeter problems by the end of the month* is specific.

(Before putting together extensive lesson plans and goals for each child, you'll want to jot down some ideas for goals for each child in different subjects.)

Goals / Reading

Goals / Writing

Goals / Math

Goals / History

Goals / Science

Goals / Socialization

Testing Options

Even if your state does not require it, you will likely want to use some type of testing. I would recommend testing even for the most casual learning methods. First, testing does not have to always include traditional pen and paper testing. Testing can be verbal or even include some type of end-of-the-unit project.

Whether it is traditional or not, testing is important because it is one aspect of measuring the success of learning. I would include a variety of written, verbal, and project-based examinations at various times throughout the school year. Bloom's Taxonomy is a great way to not only test children but to use as a guideline for what they have learned on an ongoing basis.

Types of Testing to Use

Tracking Goals

Besides written and oral testing, there are several ways to track goals and evaluate progress.

- **Create a Portfolio:** Put together a file or folder for each subject. Every few weeks, take a dated sample of work and place it in the portfolio. At the end of the semester, evaluate if and how far the child's work has progressed.

- **Teach the Skill:** If a child can explain or teach the skill or topic to another child, this is an excellent indication that he or she has mastered the material. An older child may even put together an instructional guide about the topic.

- **Self-Evaluation:** Casual conversation with a child regarding what they have learned, what they liked about it, what they didn't, etc., is also a good way to determine how much a child has learned and retained about a particular topic or skill. Older children might write a brief essay about a topic before they learn it and then again after they have finished several lessons. Comparing the two essays would indicate how much they learned.

Revising Goals and Plans

After evaluation, you will need to decide if the curriculum and method of teaching you are using are working. Don't fret about what's not working. Simply re-evaluate, revise, and move in a different direction. Sometimes all you will need is a little tweaking and you will see progress. Sometimes a child just isn't ready for a particular skill yet since each individual will learn and retain information at his or her own pace.

If, however, you decide the curriculum or method of instruction is not working, there are several steps you can take to ease into another method or curriculum.

- **Take a Break:** If you are near the end of the semester or school year, take a break from formal instruction. This does not mean a child will stop learning. Take more field trips, engage in more hands-on learning projects, or implement some more online learning options until you can figure out a new approach.

- **Join a Co-op:** If you are not already networking with other families, now is a good time to start. You might want to join a co-op just for a particular subject that doesn't seem to be working for your child right now.

- **Change Curriculum:** This is the beauty of homeschooling. You can stop something and start something new at any point during the year or the learning process. You may be able to sell your curriculum online or through a co-op to defer the expenses of investing in a new one.

Making Daily/Weekly Schedules

It will probably be easier to make and stick to a weekly schedule than a daily one. Many of us tend to be overly ambitious with daily schedules. Whether you use an actual physical planner or one online, you should write out at least a loose weekly schedule. This would generally include what you will teach, when you will teach it, and what methods and materials you will use.

Making Lesson Plans

How and when you make lesson plans will largely depend on the method of teaching you use and the curriculum you choose. Many curriculums will provide detailed lesson plans already completed. Some, however, will not. I personally love the old-fashioned ELAN weekly lesson plan books. These are physical planners with five vertical blocks listing the days of the week, Monday through Friday, along the left side of the planner. Across the top, there are eight blocks for different subjects and activities. These normally are found on Amazon for less than $20.

Specific lesson plans will often be based on educational plans and goals. Whatever goals you may have for the week, month, or semester, you will build your lesson plans around them. If learning about the Civil War is one of your goals, lesson plans might include reading a book on the Civil War, starting an art project recreating a fort or battlefield, studying generals, and visiting a historical site.

Teaching Multiple Ages

Teaching several ages takes more work and organization, but once you are in a routine, it is not that difficult. First, find out where each child is academically in each subject. Chapter Seven explains what each child should learn at every grade level and age. Some of your children, even though they are different ages, might be at the same level in math while at different levels in reading and language arts.

Start each day with group time. This might include reading books or working on a project that is appropriate for all ages. During the initial group time, loosely lay out what each child will work on for the day. When teaching a new lesson or working directly with one child, have solo work ready for other children. Whether it is books, art projects, or review worksheets, children should always have solo activities they can work on if necessary.

Teaching an Only Child

In some ways, teaching an only child is easier than managing several children and creating different lesson plans to meet each child's educational needs. You can truly work one-on-one with your child and craft an individualized learning environment. The biggest concern is probably socialization. But with all the different options and activities now associated with homeschooling, this should not be a problem. Do not let well-meaning friends or relatives tell you it's wrong or that you can't homeschool an only child. This just is not true. The following are ways to include lots of social interaction for your child.

- **Join a Co-op:** Yes, I mention co-ops a lot, but there are so many types and they are so versatile that you are bound to find one that meets your child's needs.

- **Online Classes:** There are live online classes that provide real-time interaction with both the instructor and other students.

- **Extracurricular:** Whether it is joining a music group, a sports club, or scouting, there are dozens, if not hundreds, of extracurricular activities to join, providing plenty of social interaction.

- **Part-time Public/Private School:** If your child is in high school, he or she might consider taking a few classes at a local private or parochial school.

Including Extracurricular

Extracurriculars can, and should, go well beyond the basic music, art, and gym classes. Depending on where you live and what activities are available through the community or a homeschool co-op, the options for extracurricular activities are almost endless.

How to Start a Homeschool Co-op

Co-ops help families share teaching responsibilities while increasing socialization and extracurricular activities for their children outside of the public school system. You can either join an existing co-op or start one of your own. Unless you live in a very remote area, there are probably lots of co-op options already available. Even if you are in a remote area, there are online co-ops available.

Whether you are starting a co-op or joining an existing one, you will want to start by connecting with and/or recruiting parents and families with children who are generally the same age as your kids. Newsletters and online message boards are good places to start. Most churches and neighborhood associations have online resources where you can connect with other families.

If you still can't find the right connections, type "homeschool co-op" and the name of your city or town in an internet search. Lots of information should immediately come up. If you live in a small town, you may need to type in the name of a larger town or city that is close.

When starting a new co-op, it is best to start with maybe three or four other like-minded parents. You can always grow and add more people if you think a larger group would work better. You can look in your church, your neighborhood, and among extended family and friends for people who may be interested. You will also want to consider creating a website, either to advertise for more families to join or just to have a connection spot for current families and children.

State Purposes and Goals

Like a mission statement, it is important to state a purpose and goals for creating a co-op. Are your primary goals educational? Is it to make sure your children have a solid faith-based education? Will the parents in the group split teaching duties for different subjects? Will the families pool their money and hire an instructor for a particular subject? Are the goals for the co-op more in line with providing socialization or extracurricular activities? One of the first steps when putting together a co-op is for parents and leaders in the co-op to get together and decide on these important issues.

After purposes and goals are determined, rules regarding the co-op will need to be set. How will money be handled and who will be in charge of the purse? (Will money even be involved?) Will membership fees be charged to cover costs or will you have fundraisers?

Create a Mission Statement

Write Out Purposes and Goals

Will You Have Fees or Dues?

Start Planning

Whether it is academics, extracurriculars, or socialization, you will need to start planning specific activities. Prepare a sign-up sheet for the activities that have been initially planned. Make sure each activity is gone over and approved by the person or group that is in charge.

If you have a large co-op, put a sign-up sheet on your website or newsletter for the first class or activity you have scheduled. If it is a small co-op with only a few families, you may decide to communicate through texting or even face-to-face meetings regularly.

List Ideas for First Activities

Decide Who Is in Charge

If you are starting a co-op, will you solely be leading the co-op or will there be a group of individuals with equal decision-making power? It is usually better to find a group to manage and oversee the co-op, especially if several families and more than a dozen children are involved. Whether it is volunteers or through an election process, you may want three to five individuals for an informal board.

List People in Charge of the Co-op

Decide How Frequently to Meet

Some groups may meet several times each week or only once a week. Some co-ops provide the primary educational instruction for the kids in the co-op. The times the children aren't learning as a group would be spent individually learning at home, the library, etc. Some co-ops only provide supplemental instruction and activities.

How Often Will the Co-op Meet?

Decide What Teaching Methods and Curriculum to Use

Decide what teaching methods and curriculum you will use for group learning. Information about methods and curriculum is in Chapter Two.

Teaching Methods

Curriculum Choices

Create Cohesiveness in the Co-op

Whether your group is together daily, weekly, or only occasionally, you will want to build camaraderie among your kids and the other parents. You can come up with a creative name for your group, create T-shirts, and have the kids help put out a monthly newsletter. Have celebrations quarterly or every semester to acknowledge accomplishments and hard work.

Activities for the Co-op

Co-op Options and Examples

Co-ops are described and examples are given in the previous section about different educational alternatives. We will briefly review some of the co-op examples:

- Families and kids get together for all classes each day. Parents take turns teaching different subjects, hiring instructors for all subjects, or a combination of both.

- Families and kids get together for only a few classes twice a week and might hire an instructor for some or all of these classes.

- Families and kids get together only for extracurriculars, field trips, or socialization.

Co-ops can be as simple and small as a few families taking turns teaching different subjects or as extensive as several families hiring teachers to instruct students in a church building or community center.

Pros and Cons of Co-ops

If you still can't decide if starting or joining a co-op is right for you, you will want to consider some of the benefits and drawbacks. (Many of these pros and cons were discussed in the earlier chapter on different homeschooling methods.)

Pros

- Children have access to different teachers and different perspectives.

- Co-ops can provide classes that you may feel unqualified to teach.

- Co-ops can offer extracurricular activities such as science fairs and spelling bees.

- There is an increase in socialization for both parents and kids.

- Co-ops will increase your homeschool support system.

- Children learn to follow instructions and take directions under different adult leaders with varied teaching styles.

- The variations and types of co-ops are almost endless.

Cons

- Co-ops require more conformity and are more restrictive than a single-family home school. You will have to stick to specific times and a learning structure to make it work for everyone.

- Co-ops can too easily turn into the public school classroom you're trying to leave behind. This could include grouping kids by age and too many in one group or class to receive adequate attention.

- Co-ops can be time-consuming. This can include everything from driving time and getting your kids ready to go somewhere regularly to preparing your own home and lesson plans for other children when teaching a class or activity.

- Parents might assume that in a homeschool co-op setting, especially a Christian one, bullying wouldn't be a problem. Unfortunately, all humans are flawed, and this can be an issue when you expand education beyond your own family.

- Besides bullying, sometimes parents form tighter friendships and even cliques among themselves.

While homeschool co-ops can provide many benefits, the more people and children in the group, the greater the potential for bullying, cliques, and conflict. Whether it is intentional or not, human beings are often messy, and the more you have in one group, the greater the chance that someone won't be happy.

While you generally need connection and community to make homeschooling successful, I recommend starting slow and small when beginning or joining a co-op.

Rules to Make or Consider

The following are a few questions you and your group will want to answer before starting so you will avoid any conflicts later.

- How will behavior problems be handled?

- Do parents need to stay during classes, or can they leave?

- Will classes be canceled for bad weather?

- Will there be a policy for how much notice is needed to cancel classes?

- How much will you charge if professional teachers are hired?

- Is there a refund policy for those who drop out?

Cover All Legal Bases

Each state will have different requirements regarding co-ops. For example, there might be building code requirements or fire codes to follow if several families and children are gathering in one building. If you are gathering in a church or community center, these things are probably already in place.

Chapter Six provides detailed information about the legal aspects of leaving public schools and starting or attending various educational alternatives.

Examples of Co-op Classes

The types of classes you may want to have are unlimited regarding topic and scope. Of course, you will want to cover the basics of reading, writing, math, science, and history. Chapter Seven of this book covers what academic skills children should learn and the approximate age at which these should be taught. These skills, however, can be incorporated into a wide variety of classes and interesting subject matter. The following are some classes you can have in your private homeschool or co-op for each primary subject.

- **Language Arts** – Classes on fables and fairy tales, book club classes, theatrical classes that put on Shakespeare plays, poetry classes, foreign language classes, and classes for sign language or a speech club. Start a journalism class that publishes a weekly or monthly neighborhood newsletter.

- **Math** – Classes for personal finance, computer coding, doing elaborate puzzles (study about puzzles, one-dimensional and 3-D, study the concepts related to puzzles), and classes for creating math treasure hunts.

- **Science** – Visit and study local nature habitats. Start classes on zoology, nutrition, robotics, outdoor survival skills, powder puff mechanics, destruction technology (this is learning from taking apart old appliances), and first aid classes.

- **History** – Local government study and field trips, colonial history, heroes of the faith (Corrie Ten Boom, Amy Carmichael, Dietrich Bonhoeffer, etc.), classes for map skills, and classes about holidays/cultures around the world.

- **Extracurricular Classes** – Woodworking, photography, filmmaking, Lego building, jewelry making, ceramics, scrapbooking, cake decorating, healthy cooking, canning and preserving, ballroom dancing, and cardio and conditioning.

Chapter Four

How Can You Start a School In or With Your Church?

T he following information explains how to start a school in your church or with your church. These are two different things.

The first, starting a school in your church, is simply using the building for classes, but the church itself is not officially involved in the school or the educational process. The second is when the church actually starts a school. This is a much more extensive process.

How to Start a Homeschool That Meets *IN* Your Church

Sometimes a single family or group of families in a church would like to start a homeschool and use the church facilities. There could be lots of reasons for this. For starters, their own home may not be large enough, especially if more than one family plans on homeschooling together. Perhaps they feel that the church will give their schooling a more official feel and they will be less likely to slack off or cut corners when educating their children.

In this case, the school is not officially connected to the church, the denomination, or the leadership in the church. How connected the school is with church resources, pastors, etc., can vary considerably. This is not the same as the church itself starting a school.

This initial stage of using the church facilities would include deciding if you want to homeschool just your children or work with other families. If you want to work with other families in the church, this would be similar to starting a co-op. Are there other families in your church that are already homeschooling their children? Are there families that are still in the public school system, but have expressed interest in an alternative form of education?

While it is okay to talk with other members or attendees who you think may be interested in alternative education for their children, don't wait too long to discuss this with your pastor or at least someone in a leadership position. On one hand, you don't want to go for a long period of time discussing and planning homeschooling in your church without bringing leadership on board. On the other hand, you will want to have at least a loose plan in place before bringing this to your pastor. You will need to balance your approach carefully.

Getting Ready

Queen Esther, Nehemiah, and Moses all approached their various leaders with important requests. Leaders are sometimes afraid of change, so it is important to go about this carefully. You will probably not want to approach your pastor on Sunday morning before the service. You will want to schedule a time to meet when leaders are not busy and there is time to privately and quietly discuss using the church's facilities.

- **Get Prepared** – Before approaching your church leadership, do your home-work. Prepare an appeal like you might prepare a business proposal. You want to have all your facts about starting a school, reasons for doing so, pros and cons, etc., before bringing the idea before pastors and other church leaders. Preparing and creating a solid proposal is just as important if you are a pastor and want to present the idea of starting a parochial school to your board or congregation.

- **Christian School or Homeschool?** – Some churches may struggle over whether to let homeschool families start a homeschool or co-op *IN* the church or involve families in starting an actual Christian school *WITH* the church. It may be easier to start a homeschool in the church to see how it would work on a small scale. This way, you will also find out how much interest there is in the church for alternative education.

- **How Will This Ministry Fit In?** – Even if your homeschool isn't an official church ministry, it will likely affect the church and other ministries. You may want to find a way to make the homeschool you're starting bring other ministries together, or at least support them. You want to set it up so it doesn't cause division or complicate other ministries. For example, are there other groups, such as a women's ministry, meeting at the same time you want to homeschool in the church? You will want to make sure there aren't any conflicts with scheduling or children becoming too noisy.

- **Keep Pastors and Elders Involved** – Even if your pastors agree to support your vision to homeschool in the church building and aren't going to be homeschooling themselves or actively involved in this ministry, make sure you keep them informed regarding the homeschooling process. This might include simply sending them a monthly update about what's happening in your homeschool.

Questions to Ask

It is necessary to approach leaders in your church with a general outline of how you want your homeschool to operate. You will also need answers to several questions that will affect your educational process. The following are some important issues you will want to discuss with your church leaders and other parents in the church when you are at the beginning stages of starting a school in the church.

- There are different types of insurance that churches have. Does your group need to have separate policies, such as liability insurance?

- Will the church charge your group for using the facilities, or will the building be free of charge for members and regular attendees?

- Will the church have usage restrictions for your group? This might include allowing you to use the church only on certain days and hours or restricting certain activities, food, etc.

- Will the church limit how many families/children will be acceptable to have in the church building?

- Is the school limited to using a biblical curriculum? If using a mainstream or secular curriculum, what type is acceptable?

A small homeschool with a few families in the church facility has the potential to branch out into so much more. The homeschooling families may be able to start a resource center that provides books, CDs, etc., on topics such as child discipline or recognizing gifts in children. Members of the church who have degrees or backgrounds in subjects such as math or science might put together a class for homeschooled children. This class might be held one night a week in the church and bring in people from all over the community.

These are just a few ways a small homeschool in the church could branch out and affect the church and the local community in so many positive ways. It might also be the start of the church creating a full-time faith-based school.

How to Start a Faith-Based or Parochial School *With* a Church

In this section, I specifically explain why and how churches can be involved in education. This part of the book speaks to those in church leadership positions as well as laypeople who want to initiate or become part of the process. I discuss the steps to take for a church body or denomination to start a school.

Mission Statement

Whether you're a single-family homeschooling or a large denomination starting a parochial school, you need a clear mission statement. You might think as a homeschool parent, particularly if you are not in a co-op and you are going it alone, that you don't need a mission statement. Technically, this is true. However, a statement regarding why you are homeschooling and what your general goals are will go a long way to keeping you on the right track.

If you are an individual or group starting a school in a church or with a church, you will need a mission statement. A mission statement is your central theme, idea, etc., that most everything you do in and through your school will revolve around. To give you an idea of what to include in a mission statement, the following are all points that should be included.

- You should include your core beliefs. If you are a Christian school, you might put in making disciples or raising and educating children based on biblical principles.

- You will also want to include general academic goals or what type of school culture and learning environment you want to foster.

- You might want to include the steps you will take to achieve the first two goals.

- What makes your school or academic organization unique? This could be a selling point to attract new students. It might include specialty academic classes or extracurriculars.

These are a few examples of general mission statements to help you get started.

1. *The mission of our school, in partnership with our congregation, is to empower a diverse community of students in the knowledge of God, and sound academic instruction, and to enable students to fully develop their God-given talents and skills.*

2. *In collaboration with our church family, parents, and the community, our goal is to educate students to become well-equipped followers of Christ while providing them with the best academic education possible.*

The SMART method can help you clearly define your purposes and write a well-crafted mission statement. The following is what is included for each letter of the SMART acronym.

Specific – It is essential to set a clearly defined goal or goals.

Measurable – There must be specific criteria by which to measure each goal.

Achievable – Although it may be difficult, the goals should be realistic and attainable.

Relevant – Why are the goals important to achieve?

Time-Based – There is a specific time within which to achieve the goals.

Besides a mission statement, you should probably have 1 to 3 primary goals when starting a school. There may be several smaller or secondary goals. These will likely be part of the larger primary goals. Most everything in your school should revolve around your mission statement and meeting these primary goals.

The following is a timeline of what a church needs to do before opening its school. These are general guidelines, and a school may be able to accomplish these tasks quicker, but it will normally take about a year to make sure everything that needs to be done is accomplished correctly.

What to Do at Each Stage in the Process

If you are seriously considering starting a faith-based school with a few individuals and families, a single church, a group of churches, or a denomination, you will likely want to organize a prayer team as a first step. Jesus fasted and prayed for 40 days before beginning ministry, not during or after. While I am not saying you need to fast for an extended period, or even at all, you will definitely want to get a group of interested believers together for a time of prayer.

Once it has been decided to start a school, you'll want to hit the ground running. Certain steps need to be taken as soon as possible. The following provides a general timetable of what you will need to do and approximately when each step should be accomplished or at least started.

One Year Before Opening the School

Organize a Board of Directors: Who will run and oversee the school? Will you have church leaders and elders entirely run the school? Will parents or donors be part of the board? You will want to have five to seven members on the board. Once you have a board, you can start working on or delegating the rest of the preparations on this list.

Who might you consider to be on the board of directors?

Start Doing Research: Visit other schools and note what you like and what you don't. Besides the board, you may want to put together a committee of pastors, elders, and interested parents to conduct initial research regarding what type of school you want to have, what you want to teach, and what other schools are doing.

What schools will you visit?

Gather Materials: Gather faculty handbooks, student handbooks, and office procedure manuals from schools you may want to emulate. Read and study these to have a broad understanding of how private and Christian schools operate. Begin writing your own handbooks and procedure manuals that will outline all aspects of how your school will operate.

Where will you get sample handbooks?

Craft a Mission Statement: Write a mission statement regarding what you want your school to be or accomplish. Again, study other mission and philosophy statements to help craft your own unique statement. This is important because everything you do needs to reflect your overall mission and philosophy.

What is your mission statement?

Decide Who and What You Will Teach: Decide how many grades your school will have. Are you just going to have a lower elementary school or a full elementary? Do you want a middle or even a high school? You may want to start with just a few lower grades, such as kindergarten through third grade, and add upper elementary in the second year. A few years down the road, you might want to add middle school or even high school.

What grades will you teach?

Decide About Online Education: Will you provide education totally in person, or will it be partially online? If space is limited in your church building, you may want to have at least some classes online. You might consider having students come to school part of the week and work online the rest of the time. Online platforms such as Udemy will allow you to create courses.

Will you include online education?

Evaluate Your Facilities: Where will the school be held? In the church, a building near the church, or will you need any construction of new buildings? If possible, you will want the school to be in your existing facilities. This will expose new families to your church. If new construction is not financially feasible, you may want to consider bringing in modular buildings or some other type of portable structures if more room is needed.

Is your facility adequate? Will you need new construction or use modular buildings?

Consider Your Funding: Fundraising should start as early as possible. Initial funds might come from interested parents, other churches, or businesses in the community. Grants and funds are available from the state and federal government for starting private schools. You will want to come up with fundraising ideas to implement during the year before the school officially opens. How much will you charge parents to send their children to your school? Will there be different rates for those in your congregation and those in the community? All these questions need to be answered before you start working on a budget.

List some of your fundraising ideas.

What will you charge for tuition?

Determine Your Fiscal/Tax Year: Select a start date and a fiscal or tax year. Some schools will operate from January to December, while others might select June to May. Select a fiscal year calendar that works best for your school. Make sure to include this in your bylaws.

When will your fiscal year start?

Decide on Accreditation: Will your school attempt to receive state accreditation? This will often mean that the curriculum will need to be consistent with the state requirements at each grade level. There are pros and cons to becoming accredited. See the chapter on laws and regulations.

Will your school be accredited?

Apply for Tax-Exempt Status: If your school is operating under the umbrella status of your church, you may not want or need to do this. If you decide to create a separate status for your school, you will want to apply with the IRS as soon as possible so you can solicit tax-deductible contributions. If you have an attorney, this is something you will want this professional to handle. There is more information on tax-exempt status and incorporation in the chapter on laws and regulations.

Will your school be tax-exempt?

Will your school be incorporated?

Six to Nine Months before Opening the School

Choose Teaching Methods and Curriculum: Start researching different teaching methods and curricula. Appoint a few people from the board to do this and bring samples of various teaching styles and curricula to one of the meetings. Start looking at a variety of textbooks and learning materials.

What teaching methods will the school use?

What curriculum will the school use?

Write Handbooks and Guidelines: Review your mission statement. This will be a guideline for all major decisions. You should have already started writing outlines and ideas for any handbooks and procedural manuals you plan to write. You may want to gather example student handbooks and manuals from established, successful schools. You should complete all handbooks and guidelines at least six months before your school is scheduled to open.

What handbooks will the school have?

Form Committees: Select each person on your board to head a committee that will lead and oversee a certain area. Have them form a group of volunteers if necessary. Areas might include a financial/budget/fundraising committee, a legal committee, a building & grounds committee, a curriculum committee, and a staffing committee.

What committees will you form?

Whom will you recommend for each committee?

Continue to Visit Local Christian and Private Schools: The purpose is twofold. First, to get ideas for your school, to see what they have done right or wrong, and to find out what you want to imitate and what you want to avoid. Secondly, you will want to evaluate the competition. How many private and parochial schools are in your area? Is there a specific need for certain grade levels or subjects? Also, talk to parents with children attending these schools.

How many private and parochial schools are in your area?

What have you learned from visiting these schools?

Finalize Your Facility Needs: If you need new facilities or additions to an existing one, construction should be underway. You will need to make sure you'll be able to pass all local and state codes regarding electrical, plumbing, and building regulations. Decide which rooms and areas will be used for each particular class or activity.

What buildings and rooms will classes be held in?

Are electrical, plumbing, and building codes up to standard?

Put Together an Enrollment Process: You will need an official enrollment process in place. This will need to be included on your website as well as in a paper format. (If you don't have a website, that needs to be done!) There needs to be a process for interviewing parents and paperwork that will need to be filled out.

What is included in your enrollment process?

Is your website up and running?

Start a Budget: You will want to put together a budget for your school at least six months before opening. This will include determining how much you'll charge for tuition, what you'll spend on teacher salaries, and overall operating costs. You need to find someone with experience in bookkeeping and accounting to make sure your finances are in order right from the start.

What will you charge for tuition?

What are the approximate teacher salaries?

Who will help with bookkeeping and accounting?

Start the Hiring Process: This would include contacting Christian colleges for assistance and letting local churches know. Put together an application and hiring process for how you will hire. Decide who will do the interviewing. Candidates should be approved by the entire board. You will also want to hire office and custodial staff. Hiring an administrator at least six months before opening is crucial because you need strong leadership to guide all other aspects of the process.

Who is your administrator?

What colleges or churches have you contacted?

Decide on Extracurriculars: Will your school provide extracurricular athletics, music programs, and other activities? You might want to consider working with other, more established schools to provide these opportunities for your students if you are not ready to take on extracurricular activities at this time. Another option might include partnering with local clubs and athletic organizations in your community.

What extracurricular activities will the school have?

Three to Six Months before Opening the School

Finalize the Budget: Put together your final budget and secure funding. Make sure to create a detailed budget that accounts for how many teachers, assistants, office staff, and custodial staff you will need. What is the minimum number of staff you need to get started? Keep in mind state requirements for teacher/student ratios. You will need to make these decisions at the same time you are creating a budget and determining how much you can spend during the first few years. Include supplies, curriculum, and any other costs associated with your school.

*ALWAYS create a budget that is lower than the amount of funds you expect to have. This is because unexpected costs almost always come up, especially when starting a new organization. The last thing you want is to go over budget and end up in debt your first year.

Finalize Scholarships and Financial Aid: This may be something you aren't able to offer for the first year or two. If possible, you will want to allocate part of your budget for scholarships and financial aid. This will attract more students and families who might otherwise not be able to attend your school. It is important to see a school as a ministry that not only raises children in the faith while providing an excellent education, but that can attract new people to your church.

Are you offering scholarships and financial aid? What kind and how much?

Finalize Teaching Methods, Curriculum, and Textbooks: Once this is decided, you will want to start ordering textbooks. You also need to order all supplementary materials, office supplies, and cleaning supplies. Check with OSHA and state guidelines regarding cleaning regulations.

Are curriculum and textbooks ordered?

Are office supplies and cleaning supplies ordered?

Finalize Hiring Decisions: You will want to have teaching staff hired at least three months before officially opening. This will give you time for workshops, training, and orientation. Teachers will have time to prepare their rooms and materials. Make sure all office and custodial staff are hired. Bring volunteers on board as well. If positions are not filled, does your church have individuals currently in the body who are licensed teachers? Are there individuals with clerical or accounting skills to help manage a budget?

Are all staff positions filled? What positions still need to be filled?

Finalize Facility Preparations: Any construction should be done or near completion. There will still need to be finishing touches completed to make sure everything is in working order. This goes well beyond aesthetic tune-ups. Whether it is electrical, plumbing, or even a solid roof, the last thing you want to worry about when starting a school in your church is having a lot of building repairs on top of everything else. You may want to bring in professionals to complete inspections.

Is the electrical system inspected, updated, and in working order?

Is all plumbing inspected, updated, and in working order?

Is the roof inspected and leak-free?

Prepare Furnishings: Make sure all furnishings are ready. This would include desks, chairs, and furniture for special areas such as music, art, and other extracurriculars. Office furniture and computers for offices and classrooms should be in place.

What furniture, computers, or other equipment does the school still need?

Set up a School Calendar: This will include how many days students will attend during the school year and when breaks for holidays and teacher conferences will occur. There may be state guidelines your school will need to adhere to regarding how many days each year students must be in school.

Is the school calendar in place? List start and finish dates as well as time off for holidays, parent-teacher conferences, etc.

Start to Advertise and Open Enrollment: You will want to start advertising about six months before your school opens. Advertising might include putting announcements in church newsletters, websites, and even public sites. You might want to consider newspaper and television ads depending on your budget. If your facilities are ready a few months before opening, you may want to have an open house for the public so families can see the facilities and receive information regarding your school and educational process.

What advertising have you started?

Will you have an open house? When?

Check and Confirm Regulations: Research 501(c)(3), Form 990 Schedule E, Form 5788, and Publication 557 to know which one you need or want to use. You will need an accountant and/or attorney to check your paperwork to make sure you're on board with all state and local regulations.

What forms will you need?

Do you have an attorney/accountant working on meeting regulations?

One Month Before Opening the School

Schedule a Meeting for All Staff: You will want in-service meetings for teachers and staff. This is so everyone will be acquainted with each other and on board with all school procedures and policies.

When is the school staff meeting scheduled?

Reach Out to the Local Community: Send out flyers/press releases to real estate agents in the area regarding your new school. Families moving into the community are almost always interested in school options. You will also want to try to post information in places such as a pediatrician's office or local daycares.

Where have you sent out information regarding your school?

Put Together a Daily Schedule: This should be based on the courses and classes you are offering. You should also know approximately how many students will be in each class. Your teachers should already have at least a loose daily schedule put together to share with parents.

Do teachers have their schedules and classes ready to start?

Host an Opening Night: This is different from an open house promoting your school to the public in general. This opening night is for families and students enrolled in your school. It is a time for parents and teachers to get acquainted and for students to tour the areas where they will be learning.

When is the opening night scheduled?

The next section explains how parents in a school can effectively work together.

Working with Other Parents

Networking is crucial when leaving the public school system. Whether it is other people in your church, family, neighborhood, city, or through online resources, it is extremely important to connect with like-minded individuals. Networking is defined as the process of interacting with other parents, educators, and individuals in the community to share time, resources, and expertise for the betterment of everyone involved.

The key word is share. Networking only works well if you are willing to give as much as you get. If a family continually uses other families' and professionals' time, resources, and knowledge without reciprocating, these types of networks probably won't last very long. Networking begins when you take the time to get to know other people and discover what you have in common. While most people would agree that networking is crucial for homeschool families, it is also important for those who attend a private or parochial school.

When raising and educating children outside of the public school system, there are lots of important reasons why you'll want to connect with other families. A few reasons include the following:

- Extracurricular activities are sometimes limited in small private schools. Networking can help you find and become part of different athletic, musical, and other types of extracurricular groups.

- Sharing transportation is something you will often need. In many private schools, buses and drivers are not hired to take children to various events. Finding people you trust to take turns driving with is important.

- Besides your church, places to look for networking opportunities include homeschool conventions, conferences, and book fairs. Curriculum bookstores and local libraries are other places that may provide networking opportunities.

- If you are sending your child to a private or parochial school and don't know many families, you may want to volunteer to meet new people. You could volunteer in the cafeteria or after school for extracurricular events. Maybe you have a profession or skill you could volunteer to teach students in the classroom.

List individuals or groups that are potential networking prospects.

Vouchers, Grants, and Tax Credits

I explain in-depth how families can afford to leave the public school system and how churches can financially start a school in Chapter Eight. Since vouchers and grants are an important part of starting a school in or with your church, I'll discuss these briefly here.

Vouchers: Vouchers are called school vouchers or education vouchers. Families sending their children to private or parochial schools can apply for vouchers in some states. This is a source of government funding that parents can use to send their children to a private or parochial school of their choosing. Opponents of vouchers claim they take money from the public school system, which in some aspects is true. However, most people, whether they are sending their children to public schools or private schools, are paying taxes. This tax money should go to whatever type of school each parent or family wants for their child.

Vouchers do not violate "separation of church and state." For starters, this statement isn't found anywhere in the Constitution or Declaration of Independence. Secondly, vouchers don't violate the First Amendment.

Amendment 1

Congress shall make no law regarding an establishment of religion, or prohibiting the free exercise thereof: or abridging the freedom of speech, or of the press; or the right of the people peaceably to assemble, and to petition the government for a redress of grievances.

The choice regarding where to spend the voucher money is given to individual parents – not the government. Congress is not making a law respecting religion, creating a state religion, or forcing the masses to follow any particular religion. This is about allowing individual families and parents to make decisions for their children. It is about giving parents the freedom to decide where and how to spend their tax dollars. Parents might send their child to a Christian school, a Jewish school, or any other type of school with the voucher money. Congress is not deciding where the money will be spent or how the child will be educated.

Since most parents using vouchers will likely send their child to a Christian school, this brings us to the last point that needs stating regarding vouchers – the real reasons opponents fight against them. There are generally three reasons people and organizations fight against individual freedom given to parents through vouchers.

- **Money:** The public schools and the teachers' unions have an interest in keeping most youngsters in government schools. Despite the claims often made by the unions and the media, most teachers make a good salary and have excellent benefits. Those in administration often make six figures. In many communities, the largest employer is the public school system. While it's great that families can make a good living working in education and that many local communities are boosted economically, that should not be the priority when educating our children.

- **Competition:** Public schools spend a lot of time trying to keep families from leaving and pursuing other educational options. One way they do this is by fighting against vouchers. These schools should spend as much time fixing the issues that are driving millions of families to look for alternative education. If millions of children leave, this would mean fewer tax dollars for the public schools. This, in turn, would mean that many high-paying administrative positions, teaching positions, and benefits would have to be cut.

- **Secular Society:** The Christian faith was routinely part of public education until the 1960s, when society started becoming more secular and the First Amendment was reinterpreted. Millions of families would choose to leave public schools if given a real choice that provided financial support. Many would likely select conservative Christian schools. If the next generation of children were raised with traditional, biblical values, this would almost certainly change our nation. There are some individuals and organizations that have such animosity toward Christianity and traditional values that they will do almost anything to keep that from happening.

Grants: Homeschool families can apply for grants from various sources to help cover homeschooling costs. HSLDA (Home School Legal Defense Association) has provided thousands of grants for families through the years. Finding grants for individual private school students is a bit tougher. Most of these types of grants are given at the state level.

Some people strongly support private education and homeschooling but believe taking any money from the government will bring these alternative education sources under the reign of the government with stricter guidelines and regulations. There may be stipulations when accepting grants or vouchers from different government sources. You will have to carefully look into different types of funding and decide if your family or school should accept them.

Tax Credits: *This is not legal advice. You will need to consult with an accountant or tax attorney to know exactly what you can deduct from your taxes.*

There are sometimes tax credits available and items you can write off on your taxes for homeschooling and possibly other educational alternatives. Some of this will depend on the state in which you live.

General Tips for Starting a School *In* or *With* the Church

No matter what path you decide to take when starting a school, there are some basic guidelines you will want to keep in mind.

1. Start Small – It is okay to start small with only a few families or a dozen or so students. It is sometimes better to start small. This makes your school more manageable as you learn the ropes, make mistakes, and grow in this challenging endeavor. You might decide to start as a co-op homeschool in the church building and then expand to an official school in a few years. Or you might want to start with only preschool and kindergarten, advance to lower elementary grades, and eventually have a K through 5th-grade elementary school. Unless you start with a large budget and a vast network of people and resources, you will likely want to begin on a small scale.

2. Ask for Donations – You can seek donations from your church, community organizations, and local businesses. Businesses and organizations may donate to your school in exchange for advertising. You might advertise a supporter's business in handbooks, school brochures, and some other printed materials associated with the school. Staff and students might wear T-shirts promoting businesses and organizations contributing to your school.

3. Look for Bargains – A few other ways to save money include shopping at the local Goodwill and Salvation Army for low-cost items. Garage sales and estate sales are other places to look for bargains. Everything from desks and furniture to computers and other electronic devices can often be found for a fraction of the regular cost. People in your congregation or community may be willing to volunteer their time or talents to prepare a facility and help with fundraising activities.

4. Follow All Legal and Financial Regulations/Ordinances – This is probably the least enjoyable part of starting a school, and one area you definitely don't want to cut corners on. If you can't find anyone in your church or local community who is willing to volunteer their legal and financial services, you will need to make room in the budget to hire a qualified professional.

Chapter Five

Why and How Should the Church Participate?

I have sometimes heard people in the church say things such as, "It is not the job of the church to educate the kids in the congregation. It's the parents' responsibility." This is true. But let's back up for a second and examine the primary mission of the Church.

Understand the Primary Mission of the Church

The following is a general statement that most people would probably agree encapsulates the mission of the Church.

The general mission of the Church is to spread the Gospel, make disciples, and encourage and nurture those already in the body while glorifying Christ.

A more detailed explanation of this mission would be as follows: The purpose of the Church is basically two-fold. First, to reach out into the community and lead people to Christ. We do this by meeting practical needs in various ways, such as feeding the hungry, engaging in building projects, providing services for marginalized communities, etc. This is usually how missionaries operate in the areas they hope to reach by providing hospitals, clinics, and schools.

The second part is to nurture, edify, and support those already in the body. There are many types of programs and support systems a church might develop in order to meet these needs. A school could definitely be one of these programs and support systems. Both the general purposes and overall mission of a church can be accomplished by having a school.

Most people have children. Even if they don't, most people have stepchildren, nieces, nephews, and younger cousins or siblings. Almost everyone, whether directly or indirectly, at some point in their lives is involved in the raising and nurturing of children.

A Christian school would make disciples of young children while providing quality education. It wouldn't just affect the children in the school but reach deep into the community by affecting the family members of the children who attended. It would strengthen and support those already in the body who have children, as well as those working within the school.

Another way to look at this is if the Church and the Christian community don't provide support to help their families provide quality education, the government certainly will in the form of public education. How well has this been working for us? Christianity has been dropping rapidly in the United States over the last several decades. Millions of young people either abandon their faith or adopt a watered-down, often unbiblical faith as they enter adulthood. A Christ-centered education that starts at kindergarten could help stem this epidemic of drifting away.

Charles F. Potter, who transitioned from an Evangelical Baptist to a social justice humanist during his lifetime and wrote the book *Humanism: A New Religion* in 1930, stated the following:

"Education is thus a most powerful ally of humanism, and every American school is a school of humanism. What can a theistic Sunday School's meeting for an hour once a week and teaching only a fraction of the children do to stem the tide of the five-day program of humanistic teaching?"

Most people who have been in the Church long enough know that the majority of individuals who accept Christ, initially do so as children or teenagers. I have seen numbers that state between 80 and 90 percent of believers make an initial decision for Christ before their 18th birthday. Some of these people may stray during their twenty-something and college years. Some come back and recommit to Christ, while others do not.

The point is that knowing the primary mission of the Church and that the ripest mission field is often under age 18 should convince all believers that every church should at least prayerfully consider opening a school. Starting a school, or at least supporting some type of non-public educational system, would fulfill the mission of the Church in a practical way.

Important Aspects of Homeschooling for Churches to Consider

Besides fulfilling the general mission of the Church, there are other important reasons why churches may want to take a more active role in the education process.

- Secular families are also increasingly choosing to homeschool and send their children to alternative education outside of the public schools. This provides an excellent mission field opportunity.

- With so many single-parent families, the Church can help these parents provide their children with a quality education they might not otherwise be able to give them.

- Our culture is obviously in a state of spiritual and moral decline. Even believers are finding it increasingly difficult to walk the narrow path. Churches that come alongside families through education can help support believers and their families.

- Becoming part of the educational process means connecting at a deeper level to the community around you. You will have a greater impact on not just the students and families in your school, but also the individuals and organizations throughout your entire community.

Let us examine some of the reasons believers often decide it is okay to send their children to a public school. Before delving into these reasons, I want to make it perfectly clear that I am not saying an individual is wrong or not a good parent if they ultimately decide to send their children to public schools.

Sometimes parents have taken the time to prayerfully consider their choices and have ultimately decided that is the best option for their family. Many families, however, have not really considered all their options or looked at the case for leaving public schools from every angle. The following are a few points to consider and mull over when making the best decision for your kids.

Arguments Christian Parents Often Use for Staying in Public Education

The Teacher Is a Believer

The teacher is so nice. In fact, she is a believer herself. That may be true, but the fact is public school systems are generally not Christian and oftentimes anti-Christian. The curriculum is not Christian, and much of the peer influence is not Christian. Even if the teacher is a believer, most teachers have their hands tied when it comes to what they can say or do regarding their faith.

It's Okay to Allow Children to Sow Their Wild Oats

Some parents believe that sending their kids to public schools, especially when they get to middle or high school, is okay because they are going "to experiment" in life. In some churches and denominations, kids sowing their wild oats during their teenage years is acceptable. Some people think that if kids are allowed to drink excessively, experiment with drugs, and engage in a variety of sexual activities, they won't want to do these things when they're older. This belief or practice, however, is not Scriptural. Parents may think that if they do those things when they are young, they won't have any desire for it later.

Research indicates that those who were virgins when they married were less likely to be unfaithful than those who had multiple partners. Someone who was an addict or a heavy drug user will almost certainly have a more difficult time resisting drugs in the future than someone who has never used them at all. Finally, with all the crazy things going on in many schools today, sowing wild oats does not mean the same thing it did even a generation ago. We are not just talking about getting drunk and having sex with your boyfriend or girlfriend in high school anymore.

Parents Want Their Children Educated in the "Real World"

Honestly, this is one of the most irrational excuses parents use to keep their kids in public education. Think about this one objectively. Violence and drugs are part of the real world, but no genuinely caring parent would expose their children to a situation involving violence and drugs just so they can experience the harsh realities of life. When your child needs to learn about sexuality, are you going to show a pornographic movie? That is, unfortunately, part of the real world.

Attending a parochial school or experiencing a solid homeschool education is also part of the real world. There is no fake world. Do your children need to be around the most difficult or sinful situations in life to be exposed to the real world? No matter what you choose, your children will be educated in the real world. The only question is, will their experience be in the best learning environment with the best educational opportunities possible?

Christian Students Are Salt and Light in Public Education

Parents often argue that Jesus told us to be in the world but not of the world. This statement is based on Scripture, but in this case likely misapplied. Many youngsters do not have the experience and the spiritual maturity to effectively handle situations that may come up in a secular school system. Missionaries often spend months, if not years, in education and training before churches send them to the mission field. Parents, however, often believe that kids will have the ability to effectively share their faith in a system that does not promote Christianity and is sometimes hostile toward it.

Many studies reveal that more young people are turning to secularism or the occult than are deciding to follow Christ. Take a moment to examine what is happening in our current culture and even in many of our churches. Is sending our kids to government-run schools leading thousands to Christ and changing the atmosphere in our society? Of course, there are always exceptions. There are likely cases in which God uses children to promote Christian truth in public schools. Overall, however, the evidence seems to show that this isn't the best way to reach other children while at the same time keeping our own youngsters grounded in traditional faith.

Four Reasons Why the Church Should Be Involved in Education

Raising children is the parents' responsibility, not the community's, not the government's, not the village's, not even the Church's. But I do believe the Church needs to take a more direct and active role in what is basically part of children's ministry. In conclusion, I will summarize why I believe every church should at least prayerfully consider starting a school, working in conjunction with other churches to start a school, or supporting homeschooling in their individual church and church building.

Fulfill the Mission of the Church

If the primary mission of the Church is to bring people to Christ, train them up as disciples, and send them out into the community, having a school would be one of the best ways to accomplish this, as well as provide a useful and practical service to both the body of believers and the larger community.

Take a survey in your own church to see at what age most people made a decision regarding Christ. Knowing the mission of the Church and that the ripest mission field is often to bring in believers as children, that should convince every church that one of their primary ministries should be a school. Starting a school, or at least strongly supporting homeschooling, would be fulfilling the mission of the Church in a practical way.

Proactive Ministry

This could be compared to preventive medicine. Think of all the problems we have in our communities, and even the Church – drug problems, porn addictions, divorce, and single parenthood. Statistically, we sometimes have just as many of these problems among church people as the unchurched. Why? Because the Church used to influence society. Now, society and the culture have seeped into the Church. In some cases, the American Church has grown weak, watered-down, and has caved into the culture.

To think that exposing children to 40 to 50 hours a week for 13 years in a secular school system does not have a major impact is just plain silly. Having a Christian school won't guarantee that people still won't struggle with these problems, but it will likely reduce them, and those who do struggle with these issues will have coping mechanisms that the world just doesn't offer. If the Church really wants to help people and change their lives, here is a novel idea: why don't we raise kids to be solid, mature Christians throughout their entire childhood? We just might save people a lot of misery. Christian schools are a proactive ministry.

Doing Life Together

For years, Evangelical churches have been trying to get their members to spend time together and grow as a community outside of the church walls. Besides their jobs, what do most people spend their time doing? Raising their children. If many of our people are working together five days a week, educating their children, that will automatically increase their time together and build stronger bonds and communities.

Church Hopping

A lot of churches are, unfortunately, known for their revolving door. Many people just do not stay committed to the same church for the majority of their lives as they used to years ago. Catholics and Lutherans don't seem to have the same revolving door problem that many Protestant and especially Evangelical churches do.

In the city I live in, these people seem to have a bond to one another, and they rarely switch churches. What is the difference? Many Catholic and Lutheran churches have schools, at least more than the evangelical churches normally do. When your families are around one another five days a week, plus Sundays, a bond is built that won't so easily be broken.

When you consider what the primary mission of the Church is, that most people come to Christ before age 18, that a school is a proactive ministry that can change lives and prevent many of the problems the modern Church is dealing with, and that raising children together bonds people, it seems obvious that every church should at least prayerfully consider having a school, having a school in conjunction with another church, or at least supporting some sort of homeschool co-op or another type of alternative Christian education.

Involving the Church Is Easier Than Most People Think

There are estimated to be at least 300,000 churches in the United States. Most of them are empty 90% of the time. This means that the infrastructure for the majority of children in the country to leave the public school system is already in place.

When we consider the increasing number of problems facing our public schools, it is past time to seriously make a concerted effort in the faith community to make the most of the resources God has given us.

The following are some things a church can do on a small scale to involve homeschooled and private school kids.

- Provide volunteer opportunities and/or internships in areas such as mission projects, working with the sound and tech team, teaching Sunday School or Children's Church, and helping build and maintain websites and social media.

- Provide a church library that includes a variety of books and video resources for homeschooling and general educational purposes.

- Work with state-elected officials to expand options for churches to educate children. Work to expand voucher programs and tax credits for families.

I can already hear people saying that the Church should not be involved in politics. First of all, the word politics is vague and can encompass a lot of issues. Almost everything is political these days. If you are talking about a pastor standing in the pulpit and telling the congregation who to vote for, then yes, I would say it's probably not a good idea for a church to get involved in politics.

If you are talking about issues involving sexuality, marriage, and raising children, then these are issues a church definitely should be involved in, whether they have become political in the culture or not.

There are several options for churches and denominations to consider when deciding the best way to start a school or at least support some type of alternative education for their congregants and the community around them.

- Start a school within your own church.

- Start a school in conjunction with other churches in the same denomination.

- Start a school with nearby churches that have similar beliefs.

- Start out with an online school.

- Open the church during the week to homeschool families and homeschool co-ops.

- Create a library or resource area/study area for homeschooled families.

- Put together prayer teams to decide how to best support families with children.

Chapter Six

What Are the Laws and Regulations?

This is the part where many people lose their motivation or make mistakes that may be costly down the road. Laws, regulations, and taxes can be boring and confusing. If you are starting a faith-based school or a large homeschool co-op, you will likely have board members and those on financial committees whose job it is to handle everything from tax issues to following state regulations.

It cannot be overstated how important it is to find individuals with legal and/or accounting experience who can either volunteer or, for a reduced fee, assist in these areas. You will want to at least consult with an attorney and an accountant before starting almost any type of school with or in your church. This would also be advised when starting most types of co-ops as well. If you are simply homeschooling on your own, you will likely be able to bypass this step, but I would still strongly suggest that you join a group such as the Home School Legal Defense Association (HSLDA).

Why would individual homeschooling families need to worry about legal issues? Millions of families educate their own children without experiencing any legal problems or restrictions. For some, however, issues do arise. School districts occasionally make unreasonable or even unlawful demands on families who take their children out of the public school system. Sometimes, neighbors or relatives who are hostile to homeschooling will make accusations against parents who teach their children at home.

For these reasons, you will want to at least familiarize yourself with all the laws and regulations regarding homeschooling in your state and local community. Even if you don't ever need any legal services, these groups can provide an abundance of information and resources for homeschooling families.

What Are the Laws and Regulations?

The Home School Legal Defense Association (HSLDA) is one of the largest homeschool groups in the country. It is a Christian organization, but is welcoming to all homeschooled families. Besides the HSLDA, there are other agencies and organizations that can help you determine what laws and regulations are required for the type of school you are hoping to start. The following are a few good resources to help you get started.

- Worldpopulationreview.com provides homeschool information. https://worldpopulationreview.com/state-rankings/homeschool-laws-by-state

- The Coalition for Responsible Home Education has a website for finding each state's information. https://responsiblehomeschooling.org/state-by-state/

- The U.S. Department of Education provides information about the laws in each state. https://www2.ed.gov/about/inits/ed/non-public-education/regulation-map/index.html

- Each state has a Department of Education with laws and regulations regarding different types of non-public school options. Type in your state and the words "Department of Education homeschool requirements" to find information.

The following is some general information regarding laws and regulations to keep in mind for private schools, parochial schools, co-ops, and homeschools in various states.

- Whether you are starting a secular private school, a parochial school supported by a church denomination, a faith-based school in a church, or a homeschool or homeschool co-op, the laws are primarily determined at the state level.

- Each state board of education will determine accreditation, registration, teacher certification, and licensing requirements for each type of school. Since these laws and regulations often change from year to year, I won't list any in this book since by the time it is published, they may be out of date.

- Depending on state laws, some private for-profit schools will have to obtain a Business Tax Certificate and pay a business tax. Nonprofit and religious schools may qualify under a 501(c)(3) as tax-exempt.

- Whether nonprofit or for-profit, all private schools will have to submit to local zoning, building, inspection, and public safety regulations.

- Since most churches are considered nonprofit corporations, starting a school in a church will require those operating the school to work closely with the church's board or those in charge at the denomination's headquarters in that particular state.

What Specific Laws and Regulations Should Parents Be Familiar With?

The following are a few specific items you will want to cover when starting almost any type of school.

Racial Nondiscriminatory Policy

Whether public or private, the IRS requires every school to create and publish a racial nondiscriminatory policy. Having students of various races and ethnicities is not enough to meet this requirement.

One of the requirements for doing this is to file Form 990 every year. This includes completing Schedule E. This is proof that your school is continuing to function without racial discrimination.

Some private schools are not required to file Form 990. These would include a church that has a school that is an integrated auxiliary of the church. Schools or classes that are merely an activity that the church has would be another example.

These activities and auxiliaries are required to file Form 5578 each year to comply with racial nondiscrimination requirements. What forms your school needs to fill out and file can be confusing. This is why it is extremely important to at least be a member of the Home School Legal Defense Association. You will likely want to have at least one or two consultations with an attorney to make sure you are proceeding correctly.

This nondiscrimination policy must be adopted into your board's bylaws, and written clearly in all brochures, handbooks, advertising, and admission policies. It must also be included in any scholarship application. Any official documents or written paperwork will likely need to include this.

Writing and promoting the policy is just the first step. You must practice and adhere to it in everything from providing scholarships to evaluating admissions policies, even if you do not have any minority children attending your school.

Religious Freedom

It is important to note that a faith-based private school can bar admittance based on the religious practices of a student. Private and parochial schools are allowed to practice religious freedom. If your school is promoting the Christian faith, holding worship services, and including Bible-based teaching, you are legally able to admit or not admit students on the basis of religious faith.

While you may openly be a religious institution, and in particular a Christian school, you must make sure that if you are not admitting certain students, it is because of this, and NOT based on race or ethnicity.

To make sure you are protected when admitting or not admitting students based on faith, you will need to make sure this is clearly stated and documented in your articles of incorporation. Articles of incorporation are formal documents filed with various government agencies that legally document the creation of an organization, in this case, a school. Government agencies involved are normally at the state level in this case.

If you already have articles of incorporation for your church, they may need to be amended or even rewritten. You will also want to make sure your bylaws include a statement of faith to show that your school is governed by faith-based principles.

States with Many Laws and Regulations

The following states have the most stringent laws and regulations regarding homeschooling: Massachusetts, Pennsylvania, New York, Rhode Island, and Vermont. New York requires that homeschool parents submit a notice of intent to the district superintendent, meet assessment requirements, and teach mandated subjects. You must also submit an Individualized Home Instruction Plan and file quarterly reports.

States with Moderate Laws and Regulations

At the time this book was written, the following states had moderate laws for providing an alternative education for students. Hawaii, Maine, Minnesota, New Hampshire, North Carolina, North Dakota, Ohio, South Carolina, Oregon, Virginia, Washington, and West Virginia.

States with Few Laws and Regulations

The remaining states have few laws and low regulations regarding homeschooling. Texas, for example, currently does not require notification, immunizations, or specific teacher qualifications to homeschool a child. There are, however, required subjects that must be taught. Indiana has some of the most lenient homeschool laws. In Indiana, there aren't any immunization requirements, notification requirements, assessment requirements, or state-mandated subjects.

What is Considered a School?

For tax purposes, an educational organization is considered a school if it provides formal education administered by qualified teachers and staff. This includes online as well as brick-and-mortar schools. A school is expected to have a scheduled curriculum and an official enrollment for students. In Indiana, homeschools are considered equivalent to private schools that are non-accredited.

Again, every state is different, and laws change on a regular basis. The following information provides some general guidelines and laws that were available at the printing of this book. Make sure to refer to the previous resources to find the most up-to-date information.

What Steps Should Parents Take?

The following is a list of steps you will need to take in most states when taking your child out of a public school.

1. **How to Withdraw a Child From Public School** – There are several states that require parents to notify the school district before withdrawing a child. You might also be required to register your home as a private school before beginning to homeschool. You may need to notify the local superintendent's office each year that you plan to homeschool. Even if it is not a requirement in your state, it is a good idea to write an official withdrawal letter and send one to the school, one to the superintendent's office, and one for your own records.

2. **Work with Family, Neighbors, and Local Agencies** – There are parents, unfortunately, who will neglect their children when homeschooling. These cases sometimes make it more difficult for the vast majority of parents who are legitimately homeschooling their children. An individual from the local school district or even a concerned neighbor may alert Child Protective Services if they see that your child is not attending a public school. Depending on the type of relationship you have with your neighbors, you may want to tell them ahead of time about your plans to homeschool.

3. **Extracurricular Involvement** – There are plenty of choices available when it comes to extracurricular activities for homeschooled kids. What if parents still want their children to play on teams or be in groups that are part of the public school system? There are states that will allow students to participate in extracurricular activities if the student is willing to enroll in one or two classes that the public school is offering. A parent would need to call the superintendent or administrative office in each school district to find out the requirements.

4. **Online Transition** – If you are still unsure about leaving the public schools or want a smoother transition to homeschooling, you might want to consider a semester of online home education. While conducting research for this book, more than half of all states offered public, full-time online education for free. This may be a good idea for some students when transitioning to homeschooling or waiting for a new school year to start in a private or parochial school.

Should the Church Become an Incorporation?

Approximately 85 to 90 percent of all churches in the United States are already incorpo-rated. When a church (or any organization) is incorporated, it means the church legally has the same responsibilities and rights as an individual. Unfortunately, the legal climate in our country has changed dramatically during the last few decades. People file lawsuits over things today that would have been unimaginable twenty years ago.

There are several reasons why a church may want to become incorporated. After be-coming incorporated, a church may be eligible to apply for and receive grants. People and groups are often more willing to donate money to an organization that is officially incorporated. There is also the eligibility to receive special rates for mailing. These are a few of the benefits.

There are also risks of not becoming incorporated. These could include potential lawsuits and legal responsibility. For example, every member of an unincorporated church can potentially be held responsible for the criminal or negligent behavior of just one member.

Advantages of a church becoming incorporated:

- Incorporation protects employees and members of your church from personal liability. This is officially called indemnification.

- Incorporation provides eligibility to receive special mailing rates. This is a savings for some churches that will likely add up through the years.

- Incorporation provides eligibility to receive grants through various faith-based and federal foundations and organizations.

- Incorporation provides clear and transparent operational goals and guidelines to prevent conflict or confusion in the church.

Disadvantages of becoming incorporated:

- One of the primary arguments against incorporation is the argument that when the state gives the church the privilege of a certain amount of legal immunity, the state also has the ability to exercise a certain amount of control over that church. How much control the government would try to exert over your church would probably depend on the state you live in and the current leadership in that state.

- There is also the time and money that goes along with becoming incorporated and then remaining incorporated on a yearly basis. The paperwork you need to fill out can be confusing, and you may need to hire an attorney to make sure all the necessary documents are correctly prepared.

How Can a Church Become an Incorporation?

Becoming incorporated occurs at the state level. To become an incorporation, you will need to file incorporation papers, usually with the Secretary of State. Some states will have all the necessary paperwork to fill out online on their website. You will likely have to fill out paperwork annually to maintain your status.

To become an incorporation, you will want to apply for a 501(c)(3) tax status from the IRS. You will need to file the paperwork with the office of the Secretary of State in the state you live in. If possible, enlist the aid of an attorney to make sure all paperwork is filled out and filed correctly.

Your school will likely pay significantly higher taxes if not registered with the IRS as an educational, nonprofit, tax-exempt, or a 501(c)(3). To receive these exemptions, you usually must provide the IRS with your financial information and an operational business plan. Besides the services of an attorney, you will likely want to consider meeting with a certified public accountant to make sure all your financials are in order. Every school, whether it is associated with a church or not, should file with the IRS annually.

The nonprofit, church, and/or school will need to develop a statement of purpose for their organization. This statement will clarify that their purposes and goals are entirely charitable, and religious in nature.

Once the statement of purpose is crafted, a procedure of organizational operation should be established. This is a separate document that is normally called the bylaws.

Can a School in a Church Become an Incorporation?

Christian Schools (AACS)'s purpose is to promote and develop Christian education and Christian schools in the United States. They provide a voice for Christian schools, and many schools belong to this association.

Most schools in the AACS are in operation under the umbrella of a church or church ministry. Churches are automatically considered tax-exempt organizations under federal law. This is specifically found in the Internal Revenue Code, Section 501(c)(3). Churches do not need to apply for this status, as they are usually already considered tax-exempt. Therefore, most schools operating within a current church ministry automatically have the same tax exemption as the church sponsoring them.

However, some AACS schools are not operating under the umbrella of a church sponsor. These Christian schools are required to file an official application with the Internal Revenue Service to receive tax-exempt status. These schools will receive an exemption on the grounds that they are an educational or religious organization qualifying under the 501(c)(3) section of the tax code.

Should a school operating under a church or ministry consider receiving a separate tax-exempt status? There may be some situations in which you will want to obtain a separate status. The following are a few of these situations:

- **The School Needs a Determination Letter:** There may be reasons a Christian school needs an official determination letter. You can't receive this letter unless you officially register your school with the IRS. Corporate donors to your school may insist on seeing a determination letter before making donations to your school.

- **The School Needs to Be Recognized as Separate from the Church:** Most donations go through the church to get to the school. If the school has its own individual tax-exempt status, donations can go directly to the school.

- **The School Needs Separate Liability and Insurance:** Having separate incorporation and tax-exempt status can reduce the church's insurance premiums and liability risks. Since many more people and activities will often occur through the school than the church, there is a greater chance of lawsuits against the school than the church.

- **The School Wants to Receive Certain Tax Breaks:** There are some tax benefits that are only available for schools that have a determination letter and separate incorporation. Some states may provide tax exemptions to organizations that have an IRS determination letter.

Handling Taxes

This is not advice regarding taxes, only general information. For specific guidance regarding taxes, you will need to consult with an accountant or tax attorney.

According to the IRS, churches that meet the requirements of a 501(c)(3) are automatically tax-exempt. Some churches, however, will still seek formal recognition of their tax-exempt status. A nonprofit corporation used for educational purposes can also establish a 501(c)(3).

Becoming a nonprofit school also has additional benefits. Section 270(b)(A)(ii) means that tax-deductible donations can be given to an educational organization. A school with this status can receive grants and donations instead of just relying on tuition. The ability to receive grants and donations can help fund the school and lower overall tuition for families.

It is important to note that even though some organizations are educational, they still do not qualify as a school for federal tax exemption. They can still apply for tax-exempt status. These types of organizations include the following:

homeschool co-ops, ministry training schools, youth mentorship programs, correspondence seminary programs

Creating a Business Plan

A business plan is a written document that specifically defines an organization's objectives and the steps to take to reach them. This is a detailed blueprint of how the school will function for the first several years. Donors, especially large corporate donors, will likely want to see a business plan before contributing. The more detailed the plan is, the better. You will want to refer to your business plan often during the first few years to see if you are adequately following each step and making progress toward reaching each of your stated goals. The following are several items you will want to put together in a sound business plan.

- **Mission Statement** – A mission statement is essential for a business plan. This should be at least a few sentences but no more than an average paragraph. You will probably also want to include your vision for the school, how the school will grow, and where you see the school being in five to ten years.

Write your mission statement.

- **Competitor Analysis** – From a business perspective, this may also be called an industry overview. You will need to research how many other private schools are within five, ten, or twenty miles of where your school will be. What kind of schools are they, what grades do they teach, and how much do they charge for tuition?

Write your competitor analysis.

- **Strength/Weakness Analysis** – Some refer to this as the SWOT analysis. Strengths, Weaknesses, Opportunities, and Threats analysis. Strengths might include your school's location and your staff's experience. Weaknesses could be a limited budget or an inability to find qualified staff for certain positions. Opportunities may include expansion in programs or buildings. Threats might include new laws and regulations that make it more difficult to operate or a new competitor.

Strengths:

Weaknesses:

Opportunities:

Threats:

- **Services Profile** – Obviously, you are starting a school, but what specific services and products are you planning to offer? These would include specific grade levels, subjects, and extracurriculars. Are you starting a faith-based school in a church building, a parochial school supported by a particular church or denomination, or a general private school? List in as much detail as possible who your school will serve and what you will provide. A few examples might include working to meet state accreditation standards and teaching foundations in reading, writing, mathematics, and science. You may include providing access to X, Y, and Z programs and extracurriculars.

Write your services profile.

- **Positions and Responsibilities** – You will want to list every staff position you plan to fill and exactly what each of their job responsibilities will be. Your positions will likely include teachers, teacher assistants, office staff, custodial staff, cafeteria staff, and administrators. Even if you want to fill some positions, such as cafeteria and custodial positions, with parent volunteers, you will still want to list and describe these positions.

List positions and responsibilities.

- **Budget/Expenses** – This is one of the most important aspects of your business plan, especially if you are seeking funding or donations from various sources. You will want to list every expenditure, from teachers' salaries and benefits to building maintenance and office supplies.

List your expenses.

- **Tuition/Pricing** – How much will the general tuition be for each student? Will there be discounts for siblings? Will you offer scholarships or financial aid, and what will be the criteria for each? You will also want to include the payment options you will accept.

How much is tuition?

Are there discounts?

Scholarships

Financial aid

- **Sales/Projected Income** – This is an estimation based on the budget and all operating costs versus tuition, grants, donations, and any other funding you can count on. The first few years, a school may not be expected to make a profit. (It is not true that a nonprofit is not allowed to make money. They should, in fact, strive to make at least a modest profit in order to be sustainable and build a reserve fund.)

What is the school's projected income for the first, second, and third years?

- **Advertising Plan** – How much money and resources will you need to promote or advertise your school? Make a detailed list of each way you plan to promote the school. Everything from creating a website and social media advertising to promoting the school in various church newsletters or snail mail letters are ways to advertise.

In what ways will you advertise the school?

General Terms and Definitions

The following are some general terms and definitions you will want to be familiar with regarding non-profits, incorporation, and other various business terms.

Non-Profit – This is sometimes called a non-business entity. The general definition is a legal entity that operates for the collective, social, or public benefit. Non-profit organizations are legally allowed to make a profit, but the profits must be channeled back into the organization.

Unincorporated Non-Profit – An unincorporated non-profit is any association with two or more individuals pursuing a specific service or something for the public good that is not for profit. Even something as simple as temporarily raising money for a family in need would be considered an unincorporated non-profit. An unincorporated nonprofit is ideal for short-term projects.

Incorporated Non-Profit – An incorporated non-profit is a legal entity that requires a formal structure, paperwork, and a certain amount of legal compliance. A corporation enjoys limited legal liability for its members. If you are putting together something that will last more than a year, such as a school, it is likely you will want to incorporate your organization.

Incorporation – An educational corporation is formed specifically for educational purposes, not for profit. It can be public or private, elementary, high school, or at the college level. It is considered a private corporation when it is founded or supported by private individuals, funds, or endowments. It is considered a public corporation when it is founded or supported by the state or a municipal subdivision.

Purpose Clause – This simply states the specific purpose of an organization.

Dissolution Clause – This states how you will use any remaining assets for exempt purposes. This would include educational, religious, or charitable uses.

Tax-Exempt – There are over two dozen classifications of tax-exempt organizations created by Congress. A few of these include Section 501(c)(3), volunteer fire organizations, and homeowner associations. All 501(c)(3) organizations are divided into foundations and public charities.

FEIN / EIN – (Federal Employer Identification Number) is generally the same as (Employer Identification Number).

Chapter Seven

What Academic Skills Should Children Learn at Each Grade Level?

I f you are going to homeschool, you definitely need to know what children should learn at different stages throughout their education. Even if your child will be attending a private or parochial school, it is still a good idea to understand the skills they should be mastering.

Basic skills are usually called educational standards in public schools. These are simple goals that each child should meet at certain times throughout the school year. Examples of learning standards or goals are the following:

- A kindergarten student will identify and produce words that rhyme by the end of the school year.

- A first-grade student should accurately add and subtract single-digit numbers by the end of the school year.

- A second-grade student will demonstrate command of capitalizing the beginning word of each sentence by the middle of the year.

- A fourth-grade student will be able to identify and accurately use prepositions by the middle of the year.

While some standards, or skills, are different in each state, many are generally the same. Because many skills build on each other, it is important to teach them in a specific order. Even more important is to make sure that each learning standard or skill is not just taught, but mastered before moving on to new skills.

One of the biggest problems I encountered when working in the public school system was the lack of mastery of skills. Schools would often boast about their extensive instruction methods and the rigorous curriculum they used. Even though this was normally true, students often did not master or even understand the skills before they quickly moved on to new material. Retention was even lower after they had essentially "crammed" for standardized tests.

For example, when I attempted to teach long division, I discovered that many children had not mastered multiplication tables. Anyone learning long division without readily knowing multiplication facts will obviously struggle with division. This occurred regularly with different types of skills that required prior knowledge. Public schools are notorious for passing kids on whether they have mastered and retained the skills necessary to learn more difficult material.

Even if it takes longer than you had planned, make sure your children learn basic skills and objectives before going on to new skills. Once a solid foundation is set, learning new material will become much easier.

It is also important to understand that children should not be passed along from one grade to another simply because they are a certain age. This is one of the major problems with public education. Children are individuals and should learn the following skills at their own pace. However, for parents to have a general guideline of when material should be taught and mastered, children should be proficient in the following standards and skills by the end of each grade level. Remember, these are approximate times.

Kindergarten (Ages 5-6)

Reading & Grammar

- Recognize and write all the letters of the alphabet

- Make the correct sounds for each letter

- Recognize and pronounce the first 50 Dolch sight words

- Easily retell two or three main points of a short story

- Recognize and read the days of the week

- Recognize and read their name and address

Writing & Spelling

- Hold pens and pencils correctly

- Write in upper and lower case each letter of the alphabet

- Write numbers 1 -100

- Write first name, last name, and address

- Spell correctly first and last name

- Create short stories using small sight words

- Write using different items such as pencil, pen, crayon, and chalk

Math

- Understand concepts relating to time, such as yesterday, today, and tomorrow

- Understand morning, afternoon, and evening

- Count by ones, fives, and tens to one hundred

- Identify basic shapes such as squares, circles, rectangles, and triangles

- Group objects together in sets by similarities and differences

- Know odd and even numbers

- Begin simple addition and subtraction

Science

- Know the difference between the sun, the moon, and the earth

- Know and identify basic animals

- Know colors such as red, blue, yellow, orange, green, and purple

- Know and understand when they are using each of the five senses

- Know body parts such as the brain, the heart, and the lungs

- Know and identify different types of weather, such as rain, snow, and sunshine

History/Social Studies

- Know the country, state, and city they live in

- Know the first and current President

- Understand concepts regarding family, such as mother, father, grandparents, etc.

- Understand concepts regarding traffic, traffic lights, and traffic safety

Social Skills

- Be able to stand in line quietly

- Follow simple two-step directions

- Sit still and pay attention for 15 minutes

- Correctly use phrases such as "excuse me," "please," and "thank you"

- Share items with others and take turns

- Use words to resolve conflicts

First Grade (Ages 6-7)

Teaching reading is best completed through learning sight words, phonics instruction, and emphasis on vocabulary. Reading fluency and reading comprehension are two other important components. More emphasis should be placed on sight words in kindergarten and first grade since learning sight words is generally easier. The first 300 sight words are approximately 65% of the English language, and a child can quickly learn enough words to read simple text.

By second or third grade, a child should have already learned the first 300 sight words, and a greater emphasis should now be placed on phonics and vocabulary. Phonics will be able to take a child beyond simple reading to more complex reading, with the ability to sound out new words they don't already know. Reading fluency is how quickly, accurately, and with proper expression a child can read. Comprehension is understanding and applying what the child has read.

The most common lists of sight words, or what are called high-frequency words, are the Dolch and Fry sight word lists. Reading experts may state that a child should know the first 100 sight words by the end of first grade, the second 100 sight words by the end of second grade, and a total of 300 by the end of third grade. However, by learning just five sight words each week (these can be used as spelling words) a child will be able to learn the first 300 in less than two years.

Reading

- Recognize and know the first 300 sight words

- Understand the phonics process and know dozens of phonics families (A reasonable goal is to introduce 5 to 6 new sight words and 2 to 3 phonics families each week.)

- Fluently read 50 to 60 words per minute of age-appropriate text

- Answer basic comprehension questions regarding the text read

- Begin to read with expression and fluency

- Retell a story, remembering and explaining most main points

- Describe and compare different characters

- Make predictions about what will happen next in a story

- Know the difference between fiction and non-fiction

Writing & Spelling

- Clearly write their full name and days of the week

- Write and spell each of the 300 sight words

- Write a short story about a picture

- Print all letters legibly and consistently the same size

- Understand the difference between capital letters and lowercase

- Write full sentences

Language

- Write a capital at the beginning of each sentence and a period at the end

- Know how to use a period, question mark, and exclamation mark

- Know different types of sentences (statements, questions, commands, exclamations)

- Consistently put spaces between each word

- Understand the difference between consonants and vowels

- Know beginning consonant blends and ending consonant blends

Math

- Understand "left" and "right" and organize items accordingly

- Master single-digit addition and subtraction

- Know how to count to 100

- Know how to count by 2s, 5s, and 10s

- Know the difference between odd and even numbers

- Know the difference between numbers and numerals

- Recognize basic shapes

- Recognize and repeat simple patterns

- Know how to read simple charts and pictographs

- Be able to tell time on the hour

- Understand inches, yards, meters, and basic concepts of measurement

- Understand concepts of more and less

- Understand basic fractions such as one-half, one-third, and one-fourth

- Understand place value for ones and tens

- Cut simple shapes into halves, thirds, and quarters

- Recognize different pieces of money and know what their value is

Science

- Learn about and understand different types of weather

- Learn about more commonly known animals, such as farm animals and pets

- Know the planets in the solar system

- Learn about parts of the human body

- Learn the basics about matter (solids, liquids, and gases)

- Learn about safety procedures for common household appliances

Social Studies/History

- Know what city, state, and country they live in

- Learn about the importance of families and communities and how people within these groups work and live together

- Learn about occupations such as teachers, nurses, police officers, etc.

- Understand there are different traditions and cultures throughout the world

- Be able to find their country on a world map and their state on a map of their country

Social Skills

- Children should be able to plan ahead

- They should be able to problem-solve their disagreements

- Be able to complete a homework assignment and turn it in the following day

- Use materials without breaking them and then correctly put them away

- Know how to seek out help from trusted adults

Second Grade (Ages 7-8)

Reading

- Be able to regularly use phonics to learn new words

- Be able to read 70 to 90 words per minute accurately and fluently

- Be able to read with expression

- Read and comprehend the main ideas of a story

- Be able to read silently

- Be able to find evidence from a text to support their ideas

- Understand the difference between facts and opinions

Writing

- Easily write a coherent paragraph

- Know complete sentences from incomplete sentences

- Write stories with a beginning, middle, and end (with 5 to 10 sentences)

- Copy basic information from a chalkboard

Spelling

- Learn new spelling words and vocabulary words from books they are reading or that are read to them

- Break apart and spell compound words

Language

- Understand and use contractions correctly

- Know the difference between short and long vowels

- Understand and use opposite words

- Break words into syllables

- Recognize compound words and divide them into their individual words

- Know and use singular and plural words

- Understand and use synonyms and antonyms

- Understand and use prefixes and suffixes

- Begin learning different parts of speech, particularly nouns and verbs

Math

- Be able to count change for money

- Tell time to the half hour

- Read and write numerals to 100

- Be able to do double-digit addition and subtraction

- Know how to order numbers from least to greatest and greatest to least

- Begin using greater than, less than, and equal symbols

- Begin learning how to carry numbers and regroup so they can start doing more difficult addition and subtraction number problems

- Recognize and repeat patterns

- Recognize geometric shapes in real-life

- Continue learning about different units of measurement

- Begin working out basic story problems

Science

- Learn about food groups and nutritional information

- Learn about plant life, ocean life, and insects

- Study more detailed learning about animals and life cycles

- Learn about magnetism

- Learn about planet rotation and revolution

- Understand beginning concepts regarding inertia, light, heat, and electricity

Social Studies/History

- Read and understand different types of maps online and offline

- Read and understand a globe

- Learn about famous individuals such as presidents, scientists, explorers, and world leaders

- Children should take various field trips in the community, including to courthouses, libraries, museums, and businesses

Social Skills

- Know the difference between right and wrong on a basic level

- Be able to reason and concentrate on a problem

- Be able to work well in small groups

- Become more self-aware and see their weaknesses and strengths

- Understand that negative behavior can result in negative consequences

- Begin to make independent choices and express opinions different from those around them

- Respect the rights of others

Third Grade (Ages 8-9)

Reading

- Be able to read 100 to 120 words per minute

- Be able to use different strategies to determine the meaning of words

- Be able to retell a story and remember the main events in the correct order

- There should be a strong emphasis on reading fluently as well as answering more detailed comprehension questions

- Know the difference between increasingly complex facts and opinions

- Understand cause and effect

- Know how to compare and contrast reading passages and ideas

- Know the main idea in a passage, as well as several details

- Understand the characters, plot, and setting in a story

- Organize words in alphabetical order

Writing

- Be able to write a clear and sensical paragraph with at least four or five sentences

- Be able to write a traditional letter, address the envelope, and send the letter

- Should be able to write a story using several characters, a plot, and a setting

- Write a story with a clear beginning, middle, and end using details

- Should be able to write in cursive

Spelling

- Learn five to ten spelling words and at least as many new vocabulary words each week

- Spelling and vocabulary words can be chosen from a child's current reading material

- Children should be able to determine how to pronounce unknown words through phonics

Language

- Continue to learn the parts of speech, including nouns, pronouns, verbs, adjectives, adverbs, prepositions, conjunctions, interjections, and articles

- Recognize and use different types of sentences, including commands, questions, exclamations, and statements

- Understand and use lesser-known prefixes and suffixes

- Understand and use subjects and predicates

- Recognize and underline subjects and predicates in sentences

- Continue learning plurals and compound words

- Understand and use homophones and homonyms

Math

- Memorize basic multiplication facts, 1s through 9s

- Should begin learning simple division

- Should learn to add three-digit numbers

- Should learn basics regarding area and perimeter

- Should understand and be able to finish simple patterns

- Understand the relationship between multiplication facts and division

- Round numbers to the nearest 10 and 100

- Work on more complex less than, greater than, and equal problems

- Should learn to complete simple story problems

- Read bars and pictographs

- Tell time to the minute

- Understand simple fractions

- By the end of third grade, children should begin multiplying multi-digit numbers

Science

- Should learn about animal groups and the names of each baby animal

- Learn basic facts about the Earth's physical structure

- Learn more extensively about planets in the solar system

- Learn about personal hygiene and good health practices

- Learn how to collect data and record observations

- Begin to make inferences about observations

- Learn about simple machines such as a plane, wedge, lever, and screw

- Grow and study different plants

- Learn about pet care

Social Studies/History

- Learn how to complete problems using globes and maps

- Learn about different cultures as well as the community they live in

- Students should begin learning to locate states and capitals

- Should learn to translate data and other information into graphs and charts

Social Skills

- Children should be able to work together in small groups to complete projects

- Should begin to understand in more detail how choices can affect consequences

- Should be able to participate in conversations with other people of various ages

- Begin to receive and give constructive criticism and feedback

Fourth Grade (Ages 9-10)

Reading

- Be able to read approximately 130 words per minute

- Know and understand the overall theme and several main ideas of a longer text that has been read

- Be able to read a story or listen to one and then put in order the sequence of events from beginning to end

- Be able to make predictions and draw conclusions when reading a story

- Recognize and list details in a text

- Summarize a text or story into a few sentences

- Read text and draw conclusions

- Understand cause and effect

- Understand and explain greater complexity in characters, plot, and setting

- Begin reading classics such as *Alice in Wonderland* and *The Black Stallion*

Writing

- Children should begin studying and writing different types of poetry, such as haiku

- Know how to plan, draft, revise, and edit writing

- Start writing more complex creative writing

- Be able to read and critique peer writing

Spelling

- Children should be focusing on both spelling and vocabulary words each week

- Work on 5 to 10 new words each week, focusing on spelling, meaning, and how to use the words in sentences

Language

- Grammar skills should include more difficult subject and predicate use

- Understand and use irregular vowels

- Understand and use double consonants

- Understand and use idioms

- Understand and use onomatopoeia

- Understand and use analogies

- Understand and use similes and metaphors

Math

- Children should learn long division

- Understand and work problems with remainders in long division

- Understand and apply factor families in multiplication and division

- Add and subtract four-digit numbers

- Work on more complex story problems

- Work on more complex fractions and percentages

- Work on more complex problems with area, perimeter, and rounding

- Learn to write out large numbers in written form

- Learn to read and write Roman numerals

- Begin working on simple geometry problems

Science

- Students should learn about different rocks and minerals

- Learn about earth sciences such as air quality and weather patterns

- Learn about complex life sciences and details about plant and animal life

- Expand on the study of physical sciences, including solids, liquids, and gases

- Learn more extensively about the solar system

- Continue more extensive studies regarding heat, light, and sound

- Perform experiments to prove or disprove a hypothesis

- Learn how to build and experiment with simple and complex machines

- Work specifically with objects and machines that have wheels, pulleys, levers, and screws

- Learn more detailed concepts regarding electricity

Social Studies/History

- Children should receive instruction on authority and governing bodies and institutions

- Develop an understanding of how government and governmental agencies work

- Study in more detail maps and geography (using physical, geographical maps is still important in the age of technology). This type of map reading develops spatial reasoning skills and helps children read and understand symbols.

- Learn more extensively about different countries and cultures around the world

- Study the history of local communities and the state they live in

- Be able to conduct research and write essays on a variety of historical topics

Social Skills

- Children should be able to think critically and independently

- A sense of responsibility should increase at this age

- Should recognize and understand different levels of friendship

- Should recognize peer pressure and how to deal with it effectively

Fifth Grade (Ages 10-11)

Reading

- By the end of fifth grade, a student should be able to read and discuss a full-length novel such as *Holes, Bridge to Terabithia, The Secret Garden,* and *The Giver*

- Should be able to do more advanced work regarding making predictions and summarizing text

- Should understand in greater detail concepts such as cause and effect and comparing and contrasting

- Should be taught about analogies and allegories and know how to use them

- Understand and effectively use idioms in speech and writing

- Be able to sequence and order text after reading in more detail

- Be able to write summaries for more complex text

- Draw detailed conclusions from different types of text

- Understand and apply Bloom's Taxonomy to different projects

Writing

- Students should be able to write an essay in the following forms: informational, narrative, persuasive, and entertaining

- Should understand the structure of writing and be able to write an introduction, body, and concluding paragraph for all types of writing

- Should be able to begin gathering and organizing research for more extensive writing

- Begin writing essays and longer works of fiction

- Continue learning how to plan, draft, revise, and edit writing

Spelling

- At this age, an emphasis should be placed more on vocabulary than just spelling

- Every week students should learn new words, their meanings, and how to use them (Spelling, however, can be incorporated into this.)

Language

- Students should understand and use in their work the following: vowel combinations, double consonants, and plurals

- Should have a greater understanding of digraphs, diphthongs, allegory, and hyperbole

- Continue working on irregular vowels and double consonants

- Completely understand parts of speech and be able to diagram sentences

- Complete advanced work for the following: synonyms, antonyms, homonyms, homophones, idioms, and metaphors

Math

- Students should have the ability to work out advanced multiplication and division problems

- Should be able to use problem-solving strategies to solve multi-step story problems

- Should be able to add and subtract decimals and fractions

- Should be able to work with improper fractions, mixed numbers, common factors, and multiples

- Understand the relationship between fractions and decimals

- Should understand and use in story problems units of measure, including meters, inches, yards, ounces, and pounds

- Should learn probability, ratios, averages, mean, median, mode, area, volume, and circumference

- Understand and work on problems with lines, angles, and symmetry

Science

- Fifth grade science will include a more in-depth study of much of what was learned in previous grades, including studies on earth, life, and physical sciences

- Should learn about how the environment works, different geographical regions, and the use of natural resources

- The properties of motion, matter, and the transfer of energy should be expanded on

- Should learn extensive concepts regarding hygiene, personal health, and reproductive health

- Learn about diseases and how to promote good health

- Study ecology, including food chains, ecosystems, and adaptations

- Learn how to look for patterns in nature and science

- Should study robotics and machine learning

Social Studies/History

- Students should learn about major events in both American and world history

- There should be a basic understanding of the Revolutionary War, the Civil War, and World War I and II

- Should learn about each branch of the United States government and its different functions

- Should learn about local and state governments and take field trips to local government agencies and buildings

- Study the Constitution of the United States

Social Skills

- A child should be able to work well in different-size groups, with a partner, or independently

- They should possess organizational skills and be able to plan ahead and prepare in detail various events and activities

- Be able to communicate feelings, needs, and wants verbally in an adequate manner and at appropriate times

- Be able to identify and relate to what others are feeling based not only on their words, but on their body language and facial expressions

- Effectively communicate problems and situations from another person's viewpoint, and in essence, be able to see the world from a different perspective

Middle School (Ages 12-14)

Reading

- In middle school, students should be reading a variety of fiction and nonfiction material, including historical, biographical, scientific, and technical writing

- They should be able to research a variety of sources and determine if the research is credible

- Students should possess increasingly sophisticated reading skills, such as knowing when and how to scan headlines and skim text, analyze text and make inferences, and write a synopsis for a variety of texts

Writing

- Writing should include writing opinion papers with detailed arguments and sources to support their positions

- Should learn about and know how to write specific types of essays, such as descriptive essays, argumentative essays, persuasive essays, narrative essays, and expository essays

- Should be able to write an argument using reasons and logic

- Should be able to write descriptive narratives that include a variety of details and vivid descriptions of characters and setting

- Should be able to use quotes and correctly cite research in a paper

Spelling – Spelling as a specific subject is usually phased out during the middle school years

Language – Language in middle school would involve an interactive approach, focusing on how grammar and the English language are used in various reading and writing projects. Students should have a mastery of most grammar rules to create writing that is clear and well-structured.

Math

- Mathematics skills should include solving problems for X ratios and solving equivalent expressions

- Should learn to multiply and divide fractions

- Should understand negative numbers and plotting points on quadrant graphs

- Should be able to work out basic algebra equations

- Should be able to work complex, multi-step story problems that include percentages, temperatures, and division and multiplication of large numbers

- Should begin working on geometry problems, statistics, and probability

- Should also start working with rational and irrational numbers, equations with exponents, radicals, and linear equations

Science

- Instruction should include learning about living functions, including heredity and reproduction

- Students should understand technological designs and how various technologies are used in everyday life

- Should be able to identify variables, constants, and trends in different types of experiments

- Should develop and use skills such as observation, classifying, quantifying, predicting, interpreting, effectively communicating results, and then forming conclusions

Social Studies/History

- History instruction should include an introduction to the civil and criminal justice system

- Students should learn about the production, distribution, and consumption of products and services

- Should be able to find each state on a United States map and most large cities

- Should know where all continents are located on a globe and identify prominent cities such as London and Tokyo

- Instruction should also include more in-depth teaching about different cultures, other countries, and global connections

Social Skills

- Be able to control impulses and anger

- Be able to work on long-term projects with other team members

- Develop time management skills

- Develop greater interpersonal and relationship skills

High School (Ages 14-18)

Reading

- By the time students are ready to graduate from high school, they should be able to read advanced novels and both verbally discuss and write essays on what was read

- A few novels should include *The Grapes of Wrath* and *Animal Farm*

- It is important to promote well-rounded reading that includes a variety of novels, nonfiction, magazines, newspapers, and technical reading

- They should not only make valid arguments but evaluate the reasons for arguments and opinions and cite evidence that supports a particular viewpoint

Writing

- Students need to develop proofreading and editing skills

- Should be able to do extensive research for a writing project

- Should be able to write a detailed outline before beginning to write

- Should be able to draft and then edit and rewrite several times

Math

- High school students should have an extensive understanding of algebra and be able to rewrite expressions and solve one-variable equations

- Should know how to work with various types of measurement and data, such as quantitative data, categorical data, standard deviation, and randomization

- Should have experience studying each of the following: geometry, statistics, and calculus

- Should be able to solve real-life problems, such as those that involve compound interest

Science

- Students should have skills during experiments and other scientific activities that include observing, classifying, quantifying, predicting, interpreting, and communicating results

- They should also be able to control variables and form conclusions regarding experiments

- Should be able to incorporate math skills into science, such as scientific notation and dimensional analysis

- Should be able to table, graph, and analyze all data

- Should understand and know how to use various lab equipment, including a Bunsen burner, a metric ruler, the laboratory balance, and a Celsius thermometer

- Students, especially those going on to college, should have a broad background in biology, chemistry, and physics

Social Studies/History

- Students should be able to read and analyze documents such as the Constitution and the Declaration of Independence

- Should learn about their civic responsibilities and how voting works

- Should have a more detailed understanding of major events that have occurred throughout history and how they affect our current society

- Should develop historical thinking skills that include viewing historical events from multiple accounts and perspectives, analysis of documents, understanding context, making claim-evidence-reasoning connections, and using accurate sourcing

Social Skills

- Should have life skills that include basic cooking, doing laundry, and managing a budget

- Should know what steps to take when handling emergencies without their parents' help

(This would include everything from car breakdowns to a medical emergency.)

- Should be able to develop and maintain different levels of relationships

(These would include relationships between family, friends, boyfriends, girlfriends, and authority figures such as teachers and bosses.)

After reading these lists, you may have noticed that many skills are taught at two or more grade levels. Skills must be repeated to be reinforced and retained, and then built upon to gain more advanced skills. For example, in first grade children are taught single-digit addition. By second grade, addition expands to double-digit numbers. By third grade, children learn to carry numbers when adding. By fourth and fifth grade, they should be able to add multiple numbers and large numbers. This progression of a skill is why learning and retaining each skill is so important.

Chapter Eight

How Can You Afford to Leave Public Schools?

T he first thing many families will likely say when it comes to leaving public education is that they would love to homeschool or send their children to a faith-based school, but they just can't afford it. For the vast majority of families, this simply isn't true.

Most people spend money on things they don't need and too much money on the things they do need. They often do this because they don't know any better. They look around at family, friends, and neighbors and think that's just how people are supposed to live. Unfortunately, keeping up with the Joneses is alive and well in America. I've got news for everyone: the rat race is over, and the rats won.

In this chapter, we will examine the financial aspect of providing children with the best education possible by starting with the monthly challenge. What is most important is not necessarily how much money your family earns, but what you currently spend money on with the income you do bring in.

The Monthly Challenge

Start by **Creating a Budget**. This is essential whether you are a family hoping to have one parent stay home and homeschool the kids, you are joining a co-op, or you are sending your child to a private school. You might be thinking, we already have a budget, and there is no room left to pay for a private school or for one of us to stay home.

To find out if this is true, you need to take the monthly challenge. This means before putting together a budget, you need to track your spending for an entire month. You can do this digitally on your phone, or you can take an old-fashioned pen and notepad with you everywhere you go.

Starting on the first day of the month, keep a record of absolutely **EVERYTHING** you spend money on. This starts with every monthly bill your family has, such as the mortgage, the electric bill, the phone bill, the grocery bill, the credit card bill, and car payments.

It also includes recording the candy bar you bought when paying for gas, the magazine you picked up at the drugstore, and the fast food you picked up for lunch. It includes the pricey margarita you had when having dinner at the Mexican restaurant. It also includes automatic payments deducted from your bank account each month and all your streaming and subscription services.

You need to include **every single expenditure** for your entire family for a whole month. Sitting down at the end of the month and looking at the list will be eye-opening for most people. There will likely be things you will see right away that should be eliminated. An easy way to find out what to eliminate is to place all expenditures into one of two columns: wants and needs. Most wants can be eliminated.

Making homeschooling work financially or having the resources to send children to a private or parochial school almost always involves going through your budget and making sacrifices. Now that you have done this, you need to cut out the things you know right off the bat that you don't need. These are things you have gotten used to purchasing that you probably don't really need and activities you spend money on that you will likely not miss once you cut them out of your routine. It may seem overwhelming at first, but by taking it a step at a time, you can change your lifestyle and ultimately save thousands of dollars each year.

Making Large Changes

After taking a serious financial inventory of all your spending, you may be thinking, okay, I've cut a few things, but there still isn't enough money for homeschooling or a private education. Yes, there is. The rest of the chapter lists several specific ways you can save money. Implementing even a few could potentially save you thousands each year. Most of the following suggestions for cutting expenses are likely ideas you have already heard. If you are serious about saving enough money that one parent can stay at home or you can save enough to send your children to a private school to give them the education they deserve, you will want to consider at least a few of the following.

Get Out of Debt – You have likely heard this many times before. This, however, is the first step to almost anyone's financial success, whether you are homeschooling or not. But how do you get out of debt, especially if you pay high-interest rates on loans or credit cards? You closely implement as many of the following steps as possible.

Downsize Your Home

Yes, this is a big step, but it can potentially bring in tens of thousands of dollars. Depending on how much equity is already in your home and what type of mortgage you have, the savings can be substantial. This may be easier to do if you start cleaning out unnecessary items one room at a time. Once you eliminate all unnecessary "stuff" from your home, you may realize that your family doesn't need a home as large as the one you are currently living in. Once you have cleaned out your home, don't throw anything out unless it is damaged or broken. Box and label everything so it can be sold or donated.

Refinance Your Mortgage

If leaving your current home is not an option, refinancing may be a way to lower monthly mortgage payments. Refinancing can be a complex process with a lot of factors to consider. Since this is not specifically a financial guide, I'll only touch on this. You may be able to lower monthly payments, lower your interest, and even use equity to get cash. You will need to contact an accountant or another financial professional to see if this is an option for your family.

Appeal Your Property Assessment Value

You could save on property taxes if your home has recently lost value. If you think your property tax assessment value might not reflect your home's real value, ask for a reassessment. You might also want to check what other homes in your neighborhood or on your street are assessed at to get an idea if yours seems accurate.

Re-evaluate Insurance

Most everyone carries several types of insurance policies. Homeowners, health, and car, to name a few. Insurance can be complicated, and each company may have its own way of determining rates. If possible, you should take the time to shop around for less expensive insurance. If you haven't filed any claims for a long period, you will want to ask your current insurance agent if you qualify for a lower rate. This is especially crucial for car insurance rates.

Consolidate Debt

Consolidating credit card debt is beneficial for many families. Medical debt can be a bit trickier, however. Consolidating different types of bills can streamline finances and lower interest rates. Debt consolidation is paying off several debts with a new loan. There are sometimes drawbacks, such as the possibility of increased fees during the consolidation process. It may also mean paying more interest over time if a loan is extended.

Use Only One Credit Card

Paying off high-interest cards should be a no-brainer, but since it's so easy to fall into the credit card trap, it's worth repeating. Depending on how much interest you pay each year on credit cards, this can potentially save hundreds, if not thousands, of dollars over time. Many experts advise paying off the smallest credit cards first because this will simplify your monthly expenses by having only one card to pay off. You may, however, want to pay off those with the highest interest since this will save money in the long run.

Plant a Garden

With the current cost of groceries, it only makes sense to plant a garden. Not only will you save money, but you and your family will be able to eat healthy organic food. Gardening can also be incorporated into a science project for children of all ages. Don't have a big yard or room for a garden? Even if all you have is a patio or a small balcony, you have room for a container garden.

Plan Meals and Cook at Home

Eating out is expensive, unhealthy, and doesn't necessarily save that much time. Buy in bulk, use coupons, make a list, and stick to it before shopping. Planning meals and cooking is a skill many kids today are lacking. Incorporate this into your homeschooling routine. Creating a budget for shopping is a math lesson. Selecting the foods and planning meals is both a health and home economics lesson.

Incorporate the "Eat This, Instead of That" Philosophy

Eat This Instead of That was a book that helped people make substitutions to cut calories and lose weight. The same method can be used to save money. For example, you can get plenty of protein without spending money in the meat aisle at your supermarket, buying steaks, chops, or chicken breasts. Eggs, nuts, and peanut butter are less expensive and excellent sources of protein. Canned tuna and canned salmon are also good choices that can be made into a variety of healthy, low-cost meals.

Limit Restaurant Meals

If you are tired of hearing about saving money on food, consider one more point. Averaging 15 dollars for an entrée, along with drinks and a tip, will cost a family of four at least $60 for a restaurant meal. (Probably at least $30 if you are going through the drive-thru line.) If you are picking up dinner or eating out just two or three times a week, that comes to over $5,000 a year. Switching most of these meals to dinners you cook at home will save a ton of money and improve your family's health.

Eliminate Unnecessary Subscriptions & Memberships

Newspapers and magazines are not needed if there are free or lower-cost online options. If you have a gym membership, cancel it. Walking, jogging, and bicycle riding are free or relatively inexpensive activities that are great exercise options the whole family can do together. Free weights can be purchased at garage sales and yard sales, and games such as volleyball or badminton are also good choices for simple exercise. Finally, seriously evaluate all streaming and delivery services. Most of them are likely unnecessary.

Buy Used or Generic – For Almost Everything

Whether it's food, clothing, makeup, or almost everything else, name brands are almost always more expensive and often not any better in quality. You can find good clothes, sometimes even designer brands, online and at local thrift shops for a fraction of the cost. Ask your doctor or pharmacist if any medications you are taking can be exchanged for generic brands.

Save Money on Beverages

Whether it's alcohol, coffee, or bottled water, Americans spend excessive amounts of money on beverages each year. If you do drink alcohol, don't purchase drinks in restaurants. One glass of wine in a restaurant may cost more than an entire bottle in the grocery store. Depending on the size of your family and how much bottled water you purchase in a year, you can potentially save thousands of dollars annually when drinking from the tap. Install a filtration device on your tap or filter your water through a pitcher with a filtration system. Glass is the best type of water bottle for your health. Stainless steel is also a good choice and probably the best if you are selecting water bottles for kids. Finally, brew your coffee at home. Some families spend thousands each year picking up specialty coffee and other drinks a few times a week. Eliminating all take-out coffee for a year could literally pay for a few months of tuition at a private school.

Don't Buy Disposable Products

Everything from bottled water to paper towels is expensive and unnecessary. The list would also include, but is certainly not limited to, the following:

- paper plates

- paper cups

- disposable coffee filters

- plastic baggies (These can be washed and reused if you just can't live without them.)

- regular batteries (Rechargeable batteries are an initial investment but can pay off in the long run.)

Cut the Cable and Make the Most of Free or Reduced-Cost Entertainment

Many people can't imagine not having hundreds of channels to choose from. Most of us over 40, however, remember growing up and being completely content with three or four local channels. How many people have hundreds of channels and flip through them all mindlessly because there is nothing good to watch? Even if you live in a small town, there is likely lots of free entertainment. Attend local festivals and fairs. Rent movies from the library. Enjoy local entertainment, such as high school and college plays and free concerts in parks and malls. These types of activities are normally inexpensive, and sometimes even free. They can all become part of your kids' field trips and curriculum.

Switch Cell Phone Plans

Besides signing up for automatic payments and having the most basic phone plan, there are other ways to save on your phone bill. Switching to a prepaid plan is one option, and unless you have a brand-new phone, you will want to consider dropping any insurance you have on the phone. Finally, it's not necessary to upgrade every few years. Most cell phones are built to last for several years.

Start Coin Jars

Use Mason jars, glass jugs, etc., and have one for quarters, dimes, nickels, and pennies. This is fun for kids to watch the money "grow" in the jar, and you will be surprised how quickly what you can save will add up. It is also a great tool you can use when teaching children various math or money lessons, such as how to make and count change.

Shop Thrift Stores

The Goodwill, Salvation Army, and others provide everything from vacuums and furniture to clothes and musical instruments. Many items are practically new and can be bought for a fraction of the cost in a department store. Keep in mind that a person in a third-world country will often make an article of clothing for a dollar, but by the time it goes through several wholesalers, it sells in a swanky department store for over one hundred dollars. An individual might wear it once and sell it in a garage sale for a dollar. Don't overpay for brand names and a fancy display. Buying clothes, shoes, and household items in thrift shops and at garage sales can potentially save a family thousands of dollars in a few years.

Sell Your "Stuff"

Most of us have way more material items than we need or regularly use. You likely have a closet full of clothes, shoes, and accessories. If you are like a lot of people, you probably wear only a handful of the same items that are your favorites. If you know you haven't worn something for over a year, there is a good chance you should try to sell it. You can sell items online through Craigslist or eBay. You can also have two or three garage sales throughout the year.

Practice the 30-Day Rule

Before making any large purchase (which is anything costing more than a few hundred dollars), wait at least 30 days. If you still really need the item, then make the purchase. You should allow very few exceptions to this rule. Even if an appliance such as a dryer or a dishwasher breaks down, you can wait until you find the best deal on a new one. Back in the day, people actually hung clothes on a line to dry and washed dishes by hand.

Try a Home-Made Holiday

Suggest that your family take a year off from regular store-bought items and give and receive only homemade or sentimental items. This is a time when family members can hone their talents and skills. Sewing, knitting, crocheting, creating unique crafts, and woodwork are just a few ideas for homemade gifts. You might also consider giving out coupons for mowing the lawn, painting a room, or providing babysitting for friends and family members.

Curriculum

If you are homeschooling, once you have decided what curriculum you will be using, there are plenty of options besides buying new. This is yet one more reason why you will want to join a local homeschool group. There will usually be other families who sell DVDs, books, and curricula they have already used. Online classifieds and eBay are also options for finding used curricula.

Cut the Heating and Air Conditioning Bills

Turning down the thermostat even a few degrees can save a substantial amount of money over time. You may save as much as 3% on your bill for every degree you turn down on the thermostat. Dressing in layers during colder months will keep you warm and is more comfortable than wearing a bulky coat or jacket. An interesting hack for staying cool in warmer months without air conditioning involves filling a hot water bottle with ice water and putting it in your bed. Make sure to have a separate bottle for hot and cold water since some bottles may burst when filled with hot water after holding cold.

Making Small Changes

1. Only go grocery shopping on a full stomach and without any kids.

2. Get haircuts at a local cosmetology college.

3. Limit the use of paper products such as paper towels, plates, and cups.

4. Put a dry towel in the dryer when drying clothes. This will help absorb moisture and save energy used for drying time.

5. Put a kitchen timer in the bathroom and reduce shower time to five minutes or less.

6. Utilize your local library for books, audiobooks, movies, and activities for the kids.

7. Switch from a bank that charges fees for literally everything to a credit union.

8. Use less detergent in your washer and dishwasher. Use the cold setting for most clothes.

9. Use vinegar instead of expensive cleaners for most household cleaning.

10. Take public transportation or carpool.

11. Shop on Wednesday, Thursday, or Friday. This is when most retailers roll out promotions.

How Can a Church Start a School on a Budget?

The steps for starting a school in a church or with a church were explained in detail in a previous chapter. We will now discuss how a church can start a parochial or faith-based school on a shoestring budget. Many schools are started through large denominations or otherwise have sources of extensive funding.

Many, however, who feel led to start a school, do not. There are still ways to do this even with limited funds. Although the following may not work for everyone, some new schools may be able to implement some of the following strategies.

- While you don't want to skimp on quality teachers, some may be willing to work for a lower salary for the first few years if they feel called to teach in a faith-based school.

- If you are starting small, the church may be able to find space for classrooms without having to build on or even add any furnishings.

- Consider starting with only a few grades. As the school grows, continue adding more grade levels.

- Collaborate with other churches in the area where you live. It's probably easier to do this with churches within your denomination, but it isn't necessary as long as your basic doctrinal beliefs are the same.

Ways the Church Can Save Money

A church budget must be approached with prayer, humility, and ultimately a deep trust that God will guide you through the process. There are some suggestions to consider when reigning in your church budget as well as ideas to bring in more funds.

- Start by evaluating the primary costs, which normally are personnel, facility, and office.

Write out and list your major costs when operating the church.

- Compare these costs against the vision and mission statement of your church.

Write out your mission statement and vision for your church.

- Where are you falling short? Where are you extending yourself beyond the vision?

Write down the answers to the previous questions.

- Consider refinancing any existing debt or taking a special collection to pay it down.

Does your church have debt? What options are available to reduce the debt?

- Sometimes getting outside financial help is necessary to obtain a new perspective.

Is there anyone in the church with a financial background who can volunteer in this area?

- You may need to stop or adapt certain programs and ministries. This should occur only after prayer and consultation with wise counsel.

Have you put together a prayer team or committee to review all programs and ministries?

- Evaluate each activity your church sponsors throughout the year. Whether it is in the women's ministry or a youth function, just because an activity is fun or popular doesn't mean it is necessarily spiritually edifying or meets the church's mission and goals.

List activities or programs that can be cut or modified.

- One way to review programs and ministries is to start by listing every single ministry or activity that uses church time, money, or resources. After completing the list, put together a team of three spiritually mature individuals in the church to prayerfully consider each item on the list for a week. Ask them to mark off items as they feel led. When the group gets together again, have them compare their lists.

Have you completed what is described above? Were there obvious programs or activities that everyone agreed should be cut or modified?

- Enlist the talents of the congregation. It may be possible to find everything from landscaping and cleaning professionals to providing office help and bookkeeping skills through volunteers from the church body.

Have you put together a program to enlist the services of the congregation? What does this look like?

- Cut back on services such as a church bookstore or café. If you are serving donuts and coffee before each service, consider cutting back to just coffee and water.

Are there smaller services, such as the above, that can be reduced or eliminated?

- Consider restructuring your internet or phone plans as a way to cut costs.

How can you limit or restructure internet and phone plans?

- Re-evaluate the "miscellaneous" category from your budget if you have one. If no ministry or department can claim a need for each specific cost in your budget, it might be something to eliminate or reduce.

Have you re-evaluated items on the budget that no ministry or department claims?

- Consider LED bulbs and motion sensors that automatically turn off lights.

What are you doing to cut back on electricity bills?

- Anything that might save money on electric or water bills in your home could be considered for the church as well.

Have your staff or congregation brainstorm and come up with ideas to cut back on utility bills in the church.

- Hold meetings, workshops, etc. at the church instead of at a restaurant or other off-site venue. If food is necessary at meetings, consider a church potluck instead of catering.

Re-evaluate all future meetings and workshops in the church.

- Save on supplies and postage by reaching out to members and guests through email or social media. (I love handwritten notes and cards, but when you're trying to save money, postage and paper supplies will add up.)

Are most communications in the church done through email, text, or social media?

- Partner with other churches on things such as vacation Bible camp, youth programs, and events for couples.

List some churches you can reach out to and events/activities you could partner with them on.

- Consider renting any space or unused buildings the church may own for extra income. Even renting out a shed for storage may be a possible source of income. (Yes, you can legally rent out church space. Obviously, there are some tricky aspects to this, both legally and otherwise.)

List spaces and areas in the church that you could possibly rent out.

Managing Work Schedules

Many families that successfully homeschool often have one parent staying home and teaching the kids while the other parent works full-time. While this is usually how families decide to homeschool, there are other options.

Each parent working different hours or shifts works for some families. One spouse may work full-time while the other works part-time. Others may have other family members, such as grandparents, help with homeschooling and childcare. Now that more people are working from home, some parents may be able to work at home while homeschooling. This may work out if the children are middle school or high school age and don't need as much direct supervision.

Once you decide who will work, when they'll work, and where they'll work, the next step is to put together a daily and weekly schedule. Getting and staying organized is crucial to juggling a job and educating your children.

I strongly suggest creating a weekly block schedule. You can download a block schedule template or buy a teacher planner booklet from a school supply store. You can list the hours in the day and times for different school subjects vertically down the left side of the page, while the days of the week are listed horizontally across the top. From the time you get up in the morning until bedtime, you'll want to schedule everything from each parent's work schedule and household chores to each child's school schedule and extracurricular activities.

Chapter Nine

How Can Local Communities Help?

I f you are not involved in a local church or your church is not able to provide much support for educational pursuits, you may want to turn to other groups and organizations in your community. There are various ways your local community can support alternative educational options, as well as provide your family with opportunities to bring in extra income.

Volunteer-to-Job Ideas

Volunteering is a way to support local businesses and individuals in the town or city you live in. The best way to get your community to support you and your family is to help them first. Even if they never reciprocate (Which hopefully many will!) you will still teach your children the value of volunteering, and they will almost certainly learn valuable skills they will use for the rest of their lives. The following are some ways to volunteer that can help your family connect with your community.

- **Soup Kitchen / Homeless Shelter:** Shelters almost always need volunteers. Getting to know the people in a shelter, especially the children, is a learning experience that will give your children empathy and a broader understanding of the world around them.

- **Summer Camp Counselor:** Older children can volunteer at a summer camp for valuable experience and the possibility of being promoted to a paid position.

- **Nursing Home:** There are many elderly individuals in nursing facilities who either don't have family or have relatives who rarely visit. This type of volunteering may also provide experience for a future career in a health-related field.

- **Help Build Homes:** Volunteering for organizations such as Habitat for Humanity is a great way to learn construction skills while providing homes for needy families and individuals.

- **Volunteer at the Library:** Your local library likely hosts programs that involve reading to children or teaching craft classes. Some libraries may need help reshelving books. There are usually a lot of volunteer opportunities at community libraries.

- **Volunteer at the YMCA/YWCA:** Most communities have a YMCA/YWCA that needs volunteers in various capacities. Good volunteers may be the first in line for any potential job openings.

- **Start a Mowing Service:** Middle and high school-age kids can start by volunteering to mow lawns, trim shrubs, and pick up leaves for elderly or disabled individuals. This can be a stepping stone to starting a paying business for neighbors and other individuals who see what a good job the kids have done.

- **Farming Connections on a Global Level:** The WWOOF (World Wide Opportunities on Organic Farm) is an organization that offers people the opportunity to connect with organic farmers through cultural and educational exchange.

- **Local Farming:** If you live in an area with local farms nearby or community farming in urban areas, you may want to get involved in some capacity. Volunteering or working on different types of farms are great ways for kids to learn hands-on about animals, agriculture, and how food is grown and farms operate.

- **Animal Shelter:** Volunteering at an animal shelter could be a good experience for starting a future business, such as a dog-walking or dog-sitting service.

- **Take Photographs:** Take photos during a community event. Offer the photos to the organizations involved or your local newspaper. Even though it is generally legal to take photos of people/events/etc. in public places, you will want to check your local and state laws to be sure.

- **Teach Computer Skills:** Young people with computer, internet, or social media skills can volunteer or charge a fee to teach these skills. These skills can be taught when meeting at a local coffee shop or the library.

- **Volunteer to Do Social Media:** Whether it is content creation or social media advertising, many smaller companies may be interested in volunteers or young people who can do this job for a smaller fee than hiring a professional full-time individual.

- **Tutoring:** Older homeschool and private school students may be able to tutor younger children. They may start by volunteering at a public or private school. This way, they can gain experience and make connections to the community. If they do well after a few months of volunteering, they may be able to start their own business as a tutor.

Community Groups and Businesses to Contact

Teenage homeschoolers can learn a trade and discover how the business world operates by volunteering for a local business. If your teen is dependable and hard-working, there are likely several business owners who would love to have free help.

In exchange for volunteering, the student can watch or follow the professionals in the business during slow times or other times that are convenient for the business owner. Businesses may also donate to your school or co-op in return for some advertising benefit. Simply wearing a T-shirt promoting the business when your group is on a public field trip may be enough to garner a financial donation or some other practical resource from the business.

The following are examples of businesses and professionals you might consider contacting, whether you are a homeschool, church school, or another type of private school. Young people can work or intern at these businesses to gain not only a paycheck but also valuable life skills.

- Bakeries

- Groceries

- Restaurants

- Medical Practices

- Veterinarian Practices

- Software Developers

- Computer Repair Shops

- Financial Managers

- Lawyers

- Accountants

- Hospitals, Visiting Nurses, Social Workers

- Police Officers

- Firefighters

- Florists

- Plumbers

- Electricians

- Welders

- Construction Workers / Building Companies

- Childcare Workers

- Jewelry Designers

- Gardening, Landscaping Businesses

Ideas for Starting a Homeschool Business

If you are not going to send your child to a private or parochial school but want more connection with other families than homeschooling or even a homeschool co-op may provide, starting your own homeschool business may be what you are looking for. Starting your own homeschool business would likely be one of the most challenging of all the options discussed in this book.

If you don't have the support of a church or other community organizations, you will be completely responsible for managing your children, as well as the other children who will be attending your school. You will be responsible for obtaining permits, licenses, the proper insurance, and juggling taxes and all financial issues. We haven't even gotten to the part about actually teaching students, selecting curriculum, and managing discipline. If you are still interested in a homeschool business, the following are areas you will need to cover.

- **Research Laws:** Starting your own homeschool business would be similar, from a legal standpoint, to starting a daycare in your home. You would have to investigate your state and local laws to know exactly what would be required.

- **Figure Out Finances:** Is one parent going to stay home and run the school full-time? Are two parents both going to juggle work and school responsibilities? Will you hire any outside help? Will you be applying for grants? Loans? Will you use your savings? The minimal expenditures for an at-home school business will include furniture such as desks, chairs, and tables. You will also need computers, printers, internet access, and consistent Wi-Fi. Finally, you will need curriculum, textbooks, writing, and art supplies.

- **Permits and Licenses:** Joining a homeschool group, and in particular, the

Home School Legal Defense Association (HSLDA), can provide a tremendous amount of resources and guidance. You will also want to contact your state education department for information regarding starting a homeschool business. Knowing exactly what you will be legally required to do should be your first step. You will also want to contact your state's education department to find out what types of permits, licenses, and other paperwork you need to complete to start your own school business.

- **Community Curriculum Ideas:** Hands-on learning through local businesses and community groups is a great way to supplement your curriculum and keep costs as low as possible.

Chapter Ten

Tips for Making the Most of a Child's Educational Experience

T he following are tips and ideas for improving the educational process and making your homeschool or private school experience as successful as possible.

Get Creative With Curriculum

This section is more applicable for homeschool parents who are deciding what types of curriculum their children will use. The best way to save money on curriculum, as well as having lots of options, is to network as extensively as possible. Joining homeschool groups and getting connected with other families, whether you are in a co-op or going it alone, is pretty much essential for making your homeschooling experience as successful as possible. The following are some specific ideas for saving money while finding the best curriculum.

- Shop garage sales and thrift markets for educational curriculum.

- Sell and buy items at homeschool curriculum sales, online and offline.

- Local used bookstores will sometimes carry used curriculum.

- Buy downloadable books.

- Host a buy/sell/swap curriculum party.

- If your buy/sell/swap group is big enough, sell tickets and use the money to rent a venue.

- Create a balance between printing materials and digitizing to save money on print costs.

- Scan YouTube for educational videos and general lesson content.

- Use your library for free books, resources, etc.

Promote Reading

The one factor that nearly all successful students have in common is that they are good readers. Reading, writing, and speaking are all different aspects of communicating effectively. Following the tips in this section will help your child become the best reader possible.

- Read out loud to your child several times a week.

- Have kids listen to audiobooks. Play audiobooks while in the car.

- Designate a special area in your home for reading.

- Buy books your children are interested in.

- Read comics in your newspaper and read comic books.

- Read rhymes and sing songs.

- Turn on the captions when watching TV or movies.

- Encourage children to retell stories they've read.

- Play word games. Using 3 x 5 cards, make a concentration game with sight words.

- Regularly visit the library.

- Have children write their own stories and read them out loud.

- Keep books and simple word games in the car.

- Have children put on a play about their favorite book or story.

- Don't get too concerned about reading levels when choosing books for fun reading.

Think Outside the Box When Teaching Math

You need to get creative with more than just the curriculum. Anytime you can make math into a game, you are likely to get greater student engagement. The following are some fun ways to make math more appealing for students.

- **Chalk Geometry** – Using sidewalk chalk, children of all ages can work on geometry problems. Kindergarten kids can trace objects to make circles, squares, etc. Older kids can draw and then measure the shapes, make patterns, or even intricate designs.

- **Paper Plate Math** – Write numbers on paper plates. Pass out the paper plates and then ask students to add or subtract the numbers on their plates. Have them pick the correct answer from another stack of paper plates. For example, if a child receives plates with the number 8 and the number 7 in an addition game, he or she should pick the plate with the number 15 from the second pile.

- **Plastic Bottle Bowling** – Take several empty water bottles, and with a marker or tape and paper, number each bottle. With a small plastic ball, children can take turns bowling. If they can add the numbers on the bottles they knock over, they add that to their score.

- **Map Scavenger Hunt** – Make a map of any outdoor area children must follow to find small prizes. Make maps very simple for younger children and more difficult for older kids.

- **Math Hopscotch** – Using masking tape, create large math squares with numbers inside them. Create more than one square with the same number if there are several children playing. For young children, call out numbers and have them stand on the number. For older children, call out an addition, subtraction, or multiplication problem and have the kids stand on the answer.

- **Combine Math & Writing** – Give kids sheets of paper with geometric shapes and lines for writing under each shape. Take a field trip outside, through town, the neighborhood, etc. Kids will write down where and what shapes they find in various places.

- **Paper Plate Clock** – Draw and color a clock on a paper plate. Use a split tack in the middle of the plate to attach a minute and hour hand. Children can use this to learn to tell time.

Create a Home Learning Environment

Just as children have their personal space at school, it is necessary to have this type of space at home.

- **Create Learning Spaces** – While learning occurs everywhere, not just in specified areas, it is important to have a room or space set aside for home education, study, etc. Offices and spare bedrooms are ideal choices. If you don't have an extra room, use a divider to create a separate area in the home for learning.

- **Create Personalized Spaces** – Let your children help decorate where they will study and learn. This could include choosing colorful beanbag chairs and pillows. Display artwork on walls or bulletin boards that reflects each child's personality.

- **Include Different Lighting** – You will want a well-lit space. It is a good idea to have a light or lamp that provides different lighting levels for various purposes. Brighter lights are for reading and working on math problems, while dimmer lights are okay for working on art projects or playing games.

- **Organize and Declutter** – A messy environment may be fun to play in, but isn't always conducive to learning. Try to organize materials by subject matter. Use shelves, tubs, and containers to separate and store materials for language arts, math, science, and social studies.

- **Provide Easy Access Storage Solutions** – Cabinets and containers you can't see through will make it more difficult to find items easily and quickly. Store items on open shelves and in see-through containers. Labeling shelves and containers is a good idea; just make sure to change the labels when you add or remove materials.

- **Provide Adequate Technology Tools** – While children don't need to have the most elaborate devices, they do need reliable technology. A laptop and a printer are essential. Make sure you have a stable internet connection. Adults should keep copies of all passwords.

- **Balance Technology With Traditional Tools** – We live in the internet age, and children need to learn how to use computers, research online, etc., but too much screen time is detrimental. There is even research that suggests writing things down with a pen or pencil will increase learning. There's a kinetic connection when children are using their hands to write things rather than typing or scrolling.

Chapter Eleven

Frequently Asked Questions

The Following Are Several FAQs

Does My Homeschool or Curriculum Need to Be Accredited?

While guidelines are different for each state, the short answer for both was no when writing this book. Don't allow yourself to be intimidated by anyone who claims you must have a teaching license or special accreditation to teach your children at home.

Do I Need to Have a Teaching Degree or License to Homeschool?

The answer at the time this book was published was no. Some states require parents/homeschool teachers to have either a high school diploma or a GED. Washington State currently has the most stringent standards, which require some college credits or homeschool instructors to complete a home-based study course. There are 39 states that permit parents to homeschool children regardless of their educational background.

What About Special Needs Children?

Except in extreme cases, special needs children can and should be educated along with all other children. Just as the general curriculum for homeschooling has increased exponentially during the last several years, special needs curriculum is increasing as well. Whether your child has Down syndrome, ADHD, autism, dyslexia, etc., not only is homeschooling doable, but it can also provide the personalization your child needs to thrive educationally.

As far as private and parochial schools are concerned, some schools do an excellent job of educating special needs kids, while others don't have the resources to do an adequate job. You will need to do your research to find out exactly what different private schools have to offer for your child. The short answer, however, is that it is definitely possible, and sometimes better because of smaller, quieter environments, to either homeschool or send a special needs child to a private school.

When homeschooling a special needs child, remember to maintain a balance between sticking to a routine and being flexible when necessary. It is important to note that public online schools are required to provide special needs students with specific services. Make sure your child is assessed and receives an Individual Service Plan (ISP) or Individualized Educational Plan (IEP).

Can Homeschools Apply for Grants?

Yes, there are grants at the state level that homeschool parents can apply for. Unfortunately, there aren't many options at the federal level. It is also important to note that in recent years, applications for these grants have skyrocketed, and they are normally just a few hundred dollars for each homeschooled child.

How Can I Apply for HSLDA Curriculum Grants?

The grants can help with curriculum, courses, materials, supplies, testing, tutoring, co-op fees, academic-related technology, and some diagnostic testing for special needs students. Specific criteria to receive grants may change from year to year. Below are some general stipulations you will need to follow to receive one of these grants.

- Actively homeschooled for at least three months before applying.

- You must be an HSLDA member to apply for the grants.

- Create an HSLDA account. (This is free.)

- The child or children should be between 6 and 19 years old.

- Provide evidence of significant financial need.

- Have legal custody of the child or children you are homeschooling.

- Provide contact information for at least two character references.

- Your references should not be related to you or living in the home.

- Provide receipts for how the money was spent if you receive the grant.

- Documentation for at least one month of all income and financial support.

- Diagnosis of any child with special needs.

- If applicable, the death certificate of a spouse.

- Submit a list of any materials you would want to purchase.

- Submit evidence of any military service.

Regarding the references, they should be able to vouch for your character and that you are homeschooling. The references do not need to know anything about your finances. If you apply more than once for the grant, you may use the same references in your application. The following information should be gathered for each of your two references:

- Include a full name, phone number, address, and current email address.

- Make sure the information is submitted fully and clearly so there are no delays.

What if Our Church Is Small and Can't Support a School?

If your church only has a few hundred members or less, you may not be able to start a school, at least not right away. It is okay to start small. In fact, that is probably ideal. Starting with hundreds of kids would be overwhelming. Starting with only a few and building from there means you will only need a few teachers and smaller areas to work in. You will more easily be able to experiment with what works and what doesn't. You can grow your school a little bit each year. You can also team up with other churches with similar doctrinal beliefs.

Do Colleges Accept Homeschooled Children?

Yes. Colleges are increasingly accepting homeschooled children. Parents will want to talk with admissions counselors a few years before a child is ready to go to college to find out what types of preparation individual colleges look for. Nearly all colleges look for well-rounded students. This means a student should not only have a broad academic background but also varied experience in athletics, the arts, and volunteer experience.

How Can Homeschoolers Take the SAT and Other Similar Tests?

Homeschooled students can take the SATs at a nearby college or a local high school. Most colleges will require an SAT or ACT score for admittance.

Are Private and Parochial School Teachers as Qualified as Public School Teachers?

It varies from school to school. Generally, state governments will set the requirements for private school educators. Statistically, public educators are slightly more likely to have higher degrees, such as a master's degree, than private educators. Should this concern parents? For starters, teachers with more advanced degrees are only slightly higher among public educators.

Secondly, it is important to note that success in school also has to do with several factors besides teacher effectiveness, including curriculum, class size, discipline issues, peer influence, and parental participation. Finally, there are bodies of research showing that teachers with extensive degrees and certifications aren't necessarily more effective in the classroom. If having more extensive degrees and education made a teacher more effective and had a major impact on student learning, then the public schools would not generally be underperforming private schools. According to U.S. News & World Report, private school students consistently outperform students in public schools.

Chapter Twelve

Rethinking College

How Can We Improve Advanced Education?

College is outrageously expensive and, for many students, has become little more than a four-year indoctrination camp. Many of the degrees offered are not worth the cost of obtaining them. For example, students receiving degrees in women's studies or art history will likely have a difficult time finding jobs in these fields or making enough income to make the cost of taking out loans for these types of degrees worthwhile.

Many students could find greater success going to a community college, a vocational school, or a trade school. They would leave with a more useful degree, wouldn't have the outrageous debt, and would avoid most indoctrination.

Current statistics provide dismal numbers regarding how many college grads are actually using their degrees. According to the Small Business Blog, 27.3 percent of graduates are working in the field their degree is in. This means over 70 percent are not. Even more telling is that 34 percent could have found employment in their current job without even having a degree.

The problem is that too many families still think it is a rite of passage for their kids to attend college. They may even be embarrassed if their kids don't go. Twenty or thirty years ago, it was still impressive to go to college, and not just anyone could get accepted. Not anymore.

Today, almost anyone can get into a state college, and it is still relatively easy to obtain a student loan. The only way the money train for student loans normally stops is if the student receives poor grades. But this rarely happens. Just as elementary and high school instructors increasingly pass out A's and B's for mediocre and even substandard work, college professors are doing this now as well.

Some college professors may feel guilty for failing students because of the outrageous student debt they have taken on. Some colleges may even pressure instructors to pass students because they need the stream of money coming in. Unfortunately, for many universities, it's all about the money, not excellence or student achievement. Students are basically buying a degree. It doesn't matter if a student rarely shows up for class or doesn't have any skills or understanding of the subject matter.

Parents need to readjust their mindset to the reality of what college has become. They need to stop thinking that for their kids to have a good life and a successful career, they have to go to college. That is simply not true anymore. In fact, in recent years, the opposite may be true. Kids who leave college strapped with debt may have a harder time even making ends meet.

Considering what the college system and experience have become, these beliefs are no longer true. The vast majority of kids will be better off not going through America's current university system. This is especially true if you want the following:

- Your children to maintain and follow their Christian beliefs.

- Your children to maintain and follow their traditional values.

- Your children to start out in life with little or no financial debt.

- Your children to actually obtain a good education and not far-left indoctrination.

- Your children to have marketable skills and not just a general liberal arts background.

Only a small part of college should be sitting in a classroom, listening to lectures, and doing bookwork. A general blueprint for college should be as follows:

Year One: Classroom Instruction. The first year would include classroom learning in whatever field the student majors in.

Year Two: Internship. While some internships may provide hands-on experience, in general, this type of internship will involve following around, watching, and learning from a trained professional. Students would complete two or more internships during the second year of college to get a wide range of learning experiences.

Year Three: Apprenticeship. Apprenticeship is hands-on training in a specific field. During the apprenticeship, a student would report to and have an experienced professional oversee and guide their work. There might even be a minimal amount of pay.

Nearly every profession, from teaching and accounting to nursing and engineering, could be taught using this three-year blueprint. Some careers may even require less than three years to adequately train students and prepare them for future employment.

About the Author

Stasia Decker-Ahmed is a former teacher with over fifteen years of experience in public schools. Besides *Now Is the Time to Leave Public Schools*, she is the author of several middle-grade fiction novels, a young adult novel, and a nonfiction humor book. Several of her books are written under the pen name Staz and can be found on Amazon, Ingram, and on the blog storiesbystaz.com. https://storiesbystaz.com/.

Notes

The final pages of this book are for parents, church leaders, or anyone else planning to start a school or take a child out of the public education system. This is an interactive book, with spaces throughout each chapter to jot down notes and ideas. Extra space has been provided to help you create the best educational plan for your child or start a school in or with a church.

Notes for Alternative Educational Choices

Notes for Starting a Homeschool

Notes for Starting a Co-op

Notes for Starting a School *In* a Church

Notes for Starting a School *With* a Church

Notes About Laws and Regulations

Notes About Academic Skills Children Should Master

Notes About Financing Alternative Education

Notes About Involving Your Local Community

www.ingramcontent.com/pod-product-compliance
Lightning Source LLC
LaVergne TN
LVHW051050080426
835508LV00019B/1794